Nuts, Bolts and Screws

- Hexagon Head Bolt
- Countersunk Screw
- Round Head Screw
- 'Phillips' Countersunk Head
- Split Pin
- Slotted Nut
- Lock Nut
- Grub Screw
- Grover Spring Washer
- Allen Key
- Socket Head Screw
- Square Head Set Screw
- Stud

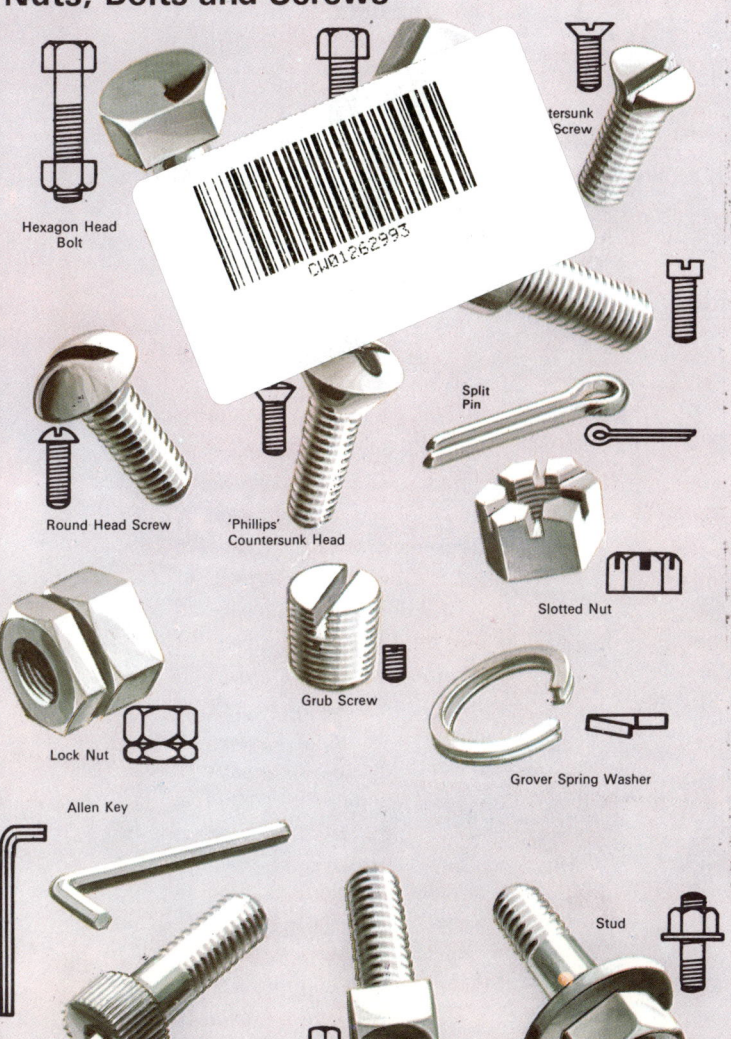

A Ladybird Book
Series 634

This carefully planned and well-illustrated book provides — at a price everyone can afford — a wealth of background knowledge and instruction on metalwork.

CONTENTS

Metals in the past	page 4
Metals today	page 6
Metals from the earth	page 8
The extraction of metals from ores	page 10
Metals and their properties	page 12
Marking-out tools	page 14
Files and filing	page 16
Saws and sawing	page 18
Drills and drilling	page 20
Soft soldering	page 22
Hard soldering	page 24
External screw threads	page 26
Internal screw threads	page 28
Riveting	page 30
Sheet Metalwork	page 32
Forging 1 (Tools and equipment)	page 34
Forging 2	page 36
Heat treatment 1 (Hardening and tempering)	page 38
Heat treatment 2 (Annealing)	page 40
Beaten metalwork	page 42/44
Casting – foundrywork	page 46
The lathe	page 48
Finishing	page 50

© **LADYBIRD BOOKS LTD MCMLXXIII**

All rights reserved. No part of this publication may be reproduced, stored in a retrieval system, or transmitted in any form or by any means, electronic, mechanical, photocopying, recording or otherwise, without the prior consent of the copyright owner.

Metalwork

by BRIAN LARKMAN
with illustrations by GERALD WITCOMB

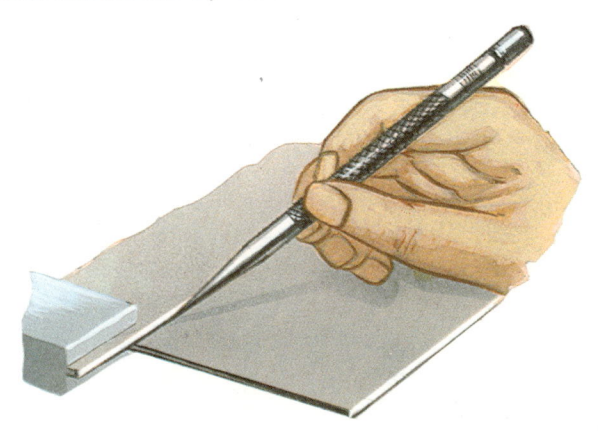

Ladybird Books Loughborough

Metals in the past

Metals have played an important part in the story of mankind. Copper was the first metal used by Man; it provided him with weapons far superior to those of stone and flint. The use of metal in battle helped to shape history. It provided spears, arrowheads, axes, swords, daggers, maces, bayonets, guns and cannons for attack, and helmets, shields and armour for defence. In peaceful times metal was used to make personal adornments such as clips, buckles, hairpins, collars and armlets. Torques were made in gold set with precious stones.

Metal ploughs, sickles, spades and hoes greatly improved farming methods. Transport relied heavily on metals for its rapid development; the railway, steamship, motor car, bicycle, air liner, hovercraft and spacecraft all needed metals.

Inventors through the ages have developed their ideas using metals. The telescope and microscope, pendulum, spring-balance, clock and calculating machine, the steam engine and the sewing machine are all evidence of Man's progress. The working of metals has been at the centre of all important technological advances.

Each age has had its metalworkers – armourers, blacksmiths, silversmiths and goldsmiths, clockmakers, toolmakers, sheet metalworkers, fitters and turners, cutlers and coppersmiths. Each new generation inherits the store of knowledge and the skills of previous generations.

History

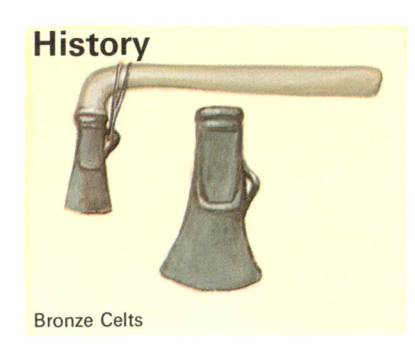

Bronze Celts

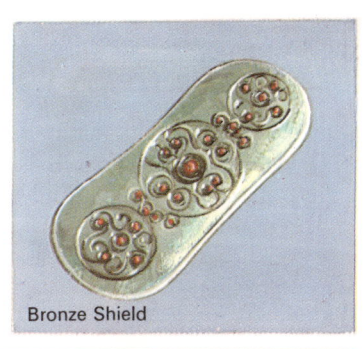

Bronze Shield

Danish Battle-axe

14th Century Cannon

15th Century Knight's Helmet

William Hedley's 'Puffing Billy' (1813)

Metals today

Metals play such an important part in our everyday living that it would be difficult to imagine what life would be like without them. With metal cutlery we eat food which is prepared in metal pots and pans on metal cookers. Our water flows through metal pipes and taps. We travel on metal bicycles, cars, buses and trains to schools, shops and offices which often have metal frames. We write with metal pens. We read books, newspapers and comics printed on metal machines with metal type. We work with metal tools. We sleep on beds with metal springs.

Today the science of metals – metallurgy – is highly developed. Man has discovered over seventy basic metals, and by mixing metals to form alloys he has made many more. For example, the metallurgist can make special metals with the particular properties needed to solve the problems posed by developments in space flight and interplanetary exploration.

Metal is an ideal material for use in mass-production because of its uniform working qualities. It can be bent, stretched, twisted, folded, cast, riveted, welded, drilled and cut with precision. Heat treatments can make metals harder or softer as the work demands. These qualities make possible the flow of cars, aeroplanes, tools, window frames, cookers, heaters and thousands of other products from the factories of the world.

The tremendous strength of metals makes possible giant projects like bridges, ocean-going tankers and oil rigs at sea. In contrast, precious metals are worked by individual craftsmen to produce unique rings, pendants, bowls and chalices of great beauty.

Racing Car

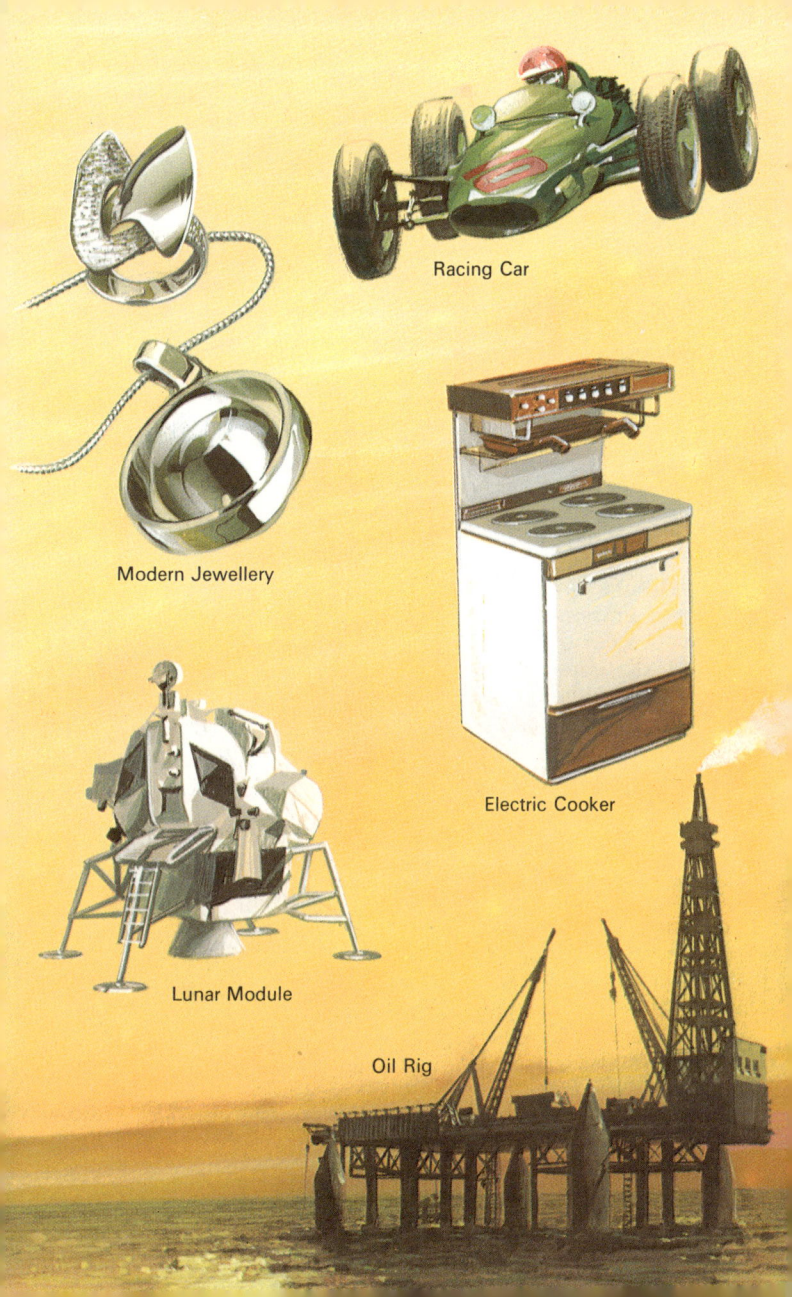

Modern Jewellery

Electric Cooker

Lunar Module

Oil Rig

Metals from the earth

Metals are widely distributed over the earth's crust but are commercially worthwhile only when found in large deposits.

Copper was probably the first metal to be discovered by Man because it exists in some places in an almost pure metallic form. Its discovery may have been made when early Man lit a fire near an exposed seam and accidentally smelted the ore, leaving behind beads of metal in the embers. Bronze, an alloy of tin and copper, was used for making tools after about 5000 BC.

Many ores are rich in copper. A sulphur compound, *chalcocite*, contains 80% copper. Iron-bearing ores like *hematite* occur very near the surface of the earth. They are mined by huge 'walking' draglines which scrape away the top-soil, dig out the ores and then replace the soil.

Tin ores are found in many areas. They can be extracted by mining from deep seams or by water-mining when they occur near the surface. In this second method, powerful jets of water wash the ore into specially constructed channels where the ore sinks to the bottom and the muddy waste is washed away. In Malaya, floating dredges are used to raise alluvial deposits of tin ore from the bottoms of lakes and rivers.

Lead is deep mined. *Galena* ore contains 87% lead. Zinc is found in the ores *zinc blende* and *calamine*.

Aluminium is the earth's most abundant metal, being a constituent of almost all common rock. The only commercial aluminium ore is *bauxite*, which is open-cast mined. The aluminium is released from the ore by using another mineral, cryolite, and an electrolytic process. This technique was developed only late in the 19th century and for this reason aluminium is often considered a 'new' metal.

A giant 'Walking Dragline', used for stripping the 'overburden' from the ore.

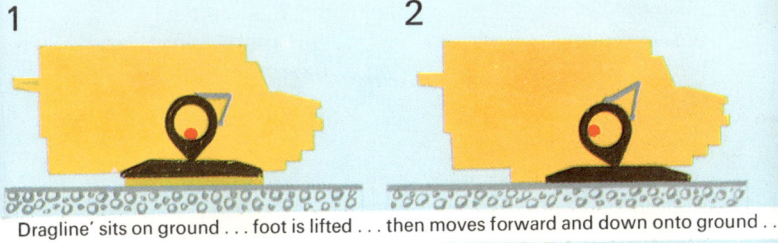

1 Dragline' sits on ground ... foot is lifted ...

2 then moves forward and down onto ground ..

3 the leg levers 'Dragline' up and forward ...

4 and one stride is completed.

The extraction of metals from ores

Producing usable metals from metal-bearing ores is called extraction. Many of the processes are very complex. Usually the ores are crushed and then smelted in some form of furnace.

The molten metal is first cast into slabs or large ingots; later these are rolled into sheets, cast into moulds, drawn into rods, wires or tubes or extruded into complex sections.

The making of iron and steel is a large part of the world's total production of metals. The process starts with smelting in a *blast furnace*. Here the iron ore is mixed with coke as a fuel and limestone as a flux. The furnace is about 100 feet (30 metres) tall and burns continuously for up to five years. A blast of air is blown into the base of the fire to produce the high temperatures needed.

Some of the iron is used directly to make castings; the remainder is refined further to produce a wide range of low carbon steels. In the *Bessemer converter* the molten iron, weighing up to 15 tons (15·24 tonnes), has air forced through it at high pressure. This burns off all the excess carbon. Much steel is now produced by *electric arc* furnaces. In these, carbon electrodes make a flash, or arc, between themselves and the molten metal, producing a temperature of 3400°C. A slag of oxide containing carbon and other impurities results which is raked off the surface of the melt.

Aluminium is extracted by an electrolytic process in a *reduction cell*. The aluminium-bearing ore, bauxite, is ground to a powder and processed chemically to produce an oxide – alumina. The oxide is put into a solution of molten cryolite at 1000°C and a very heavy current is passed between carbon electrodes and the carbon lining of the cell bath. The pure aluminium is deposited at the bottom of the bath and periodically tapped off.

Extraction

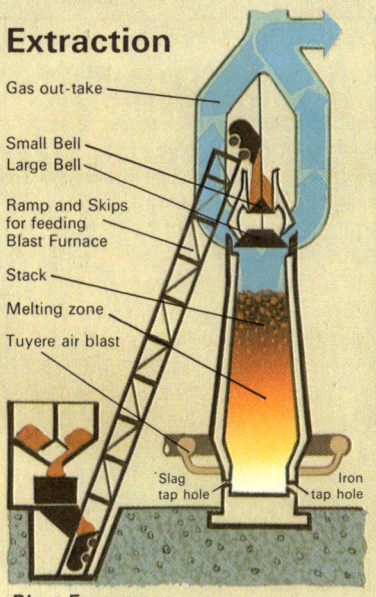

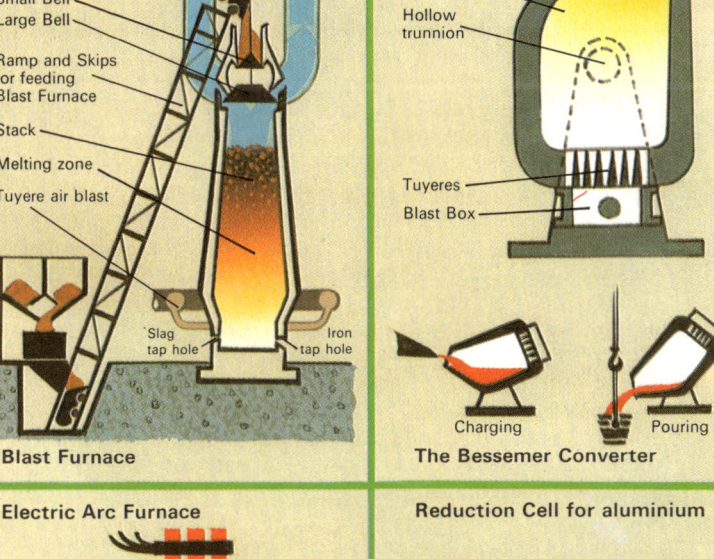

Blast Furnace
- Gas out-take
- Small Bell
- Large Bell
- Ramp and Skips for feeding Blast Furnace
- Stack
- Melting zone
- Tuyere air blast
- Slag tap hole
- Iron tap hole

The Bessemer Converter
- Bessemer Furnace in blow
- Steel casing
- Refactory lining
- Hollow trunnion
- Tuyeres
- Blast Box
- Charging
- Pouring

Electric Arc Furnace 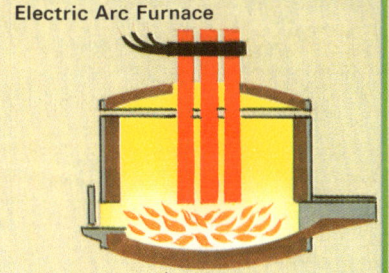
1) Charging scrap
2) Melting
3) Sampling
4) Additions
5) Slagging
6) Pouring

Reduction Cell for aluminium
- Alumina and Molten Cryolite
- Molten Aluminium

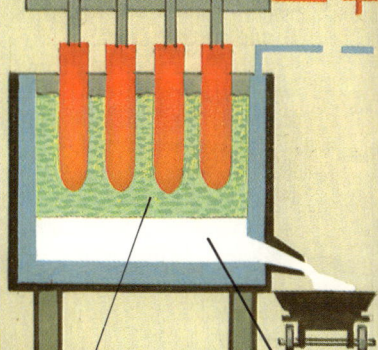

Metals and their properties

Some metals are light, others very heavy. Some are soft and easy to bend; others are hard and brittle. Each job requires the most suitable metal. To obtain metals with special properties, alloys are made by mixing base metals – bronze is made from copper and tin. Special strong, lightweight aluminium alloys have been developed for aircraft and space flight.

Metals containing iron are known as *ferrous* metals, those without iron are *non-ferrous* metals. Some of the wide range of metals available are listed below.

Cast iron – a ferrous metal of 93% iron and 3% carbon. It is very brittle under a hard skin. Used for bodies of machine tools, vices, pillar boxes, etc.

Mild steel – a ferrous metal of 99% iron and 0.25% carbon. Very tough and ductile and works well. It has a great many uses – for girders in bridges, tubes in bicycle frames, nuts and bolts, etc.

Aluminium – a pure or base metal. Very light and resistant to corrosion. It is used for cooking utensils and foil (often called 'silver paper'). Alloyed with small amounts of copper, manganese and silicon it becomes *Duralumin*, much used in aircraft.

Copper – a pure metal. Bends and stretches without fracture. A good conductor of heat and electricity. Used for electrical wiring, tubing for water supply and sometimes for roofing.

Brass – an alloy of copper and zinc, available in many varying proportions of the two metals. Brass turns well, is easily cast and resists corrosion. It is used for taps and other water fittings.

Tin – a pure metal, highly resistant to corrosion. Little used on its own but much used as a protective coating – tinplate – and in alloys.

Zinc – a pure metal which casts well and resists corrosion. Used as a coating on steel – *galvanising* – and in alloys.

Lead – is heavy and has a very low melting point. It is a pure metal which bends and stretches easily. Used in plumbing, on roofs, and as plates in car batteries.

Bar	Copper Tube	Square
Rod	Silver Wire	Gold Ingot
Girder	Aluminium Extrusion	Angle
Hexagonal	Brass Sheet	Perforated Zinc

Marking-out tools

Accurate marking-out and measuring are vital to good metalwork. Metal can be worked to very fine limits; one thousandth of an inch (·025mm) is commonplace. Many jobs consist of a number of components and without accurate marking-out at an early stage the parts would not fit.

The *scriber* is the metalworker's pencil. It has a hard, sharp point which scratches a fine, bright line onto the metal.

The *rule* is made of steel in varying lengths. It has a zero end and is calibrated with imperial or metric measurements, or both.

The *try square* is accurately set to 90° and is used for marking-out and testing right angles.

Spring dividers act like a compass and are used for drawing circles, dividing lengths and transferring measurements from rule to work.

Odd leg calipers, sometimes called jenny 'calipers,' are used for marking lines parallel to edges. *Inside and outside calipers* are used for gauging the diameter of circular parts. The tips of the legs are adjusted to touch the work gently and are then checked against the rule.

The *centre punch* is used mainly for marking the positions of drilled holes. Its mark prevents the tip of the drill from wandering.

For increased accuracy in marking-out, a *surface plate, scribing block* and *vee blocks* are used. The plate is a perfectly flat surface and measurements above it are set up on the scribing block using its fine adjustment mechanism. Precise vee blocks ensure that the work is set up at right angles to the plate. The vee-shaped grooves are to support rods for marking-out.

Metals are often painted with a quick-drying marking fluid, which is usually blue in colour, so that scratched lines stand out clearly.

The *micrometer* is a high precision tool for measuring. Each turn or part turn of its fine thread can be checked exactly against a scale engraved on it.

Rule

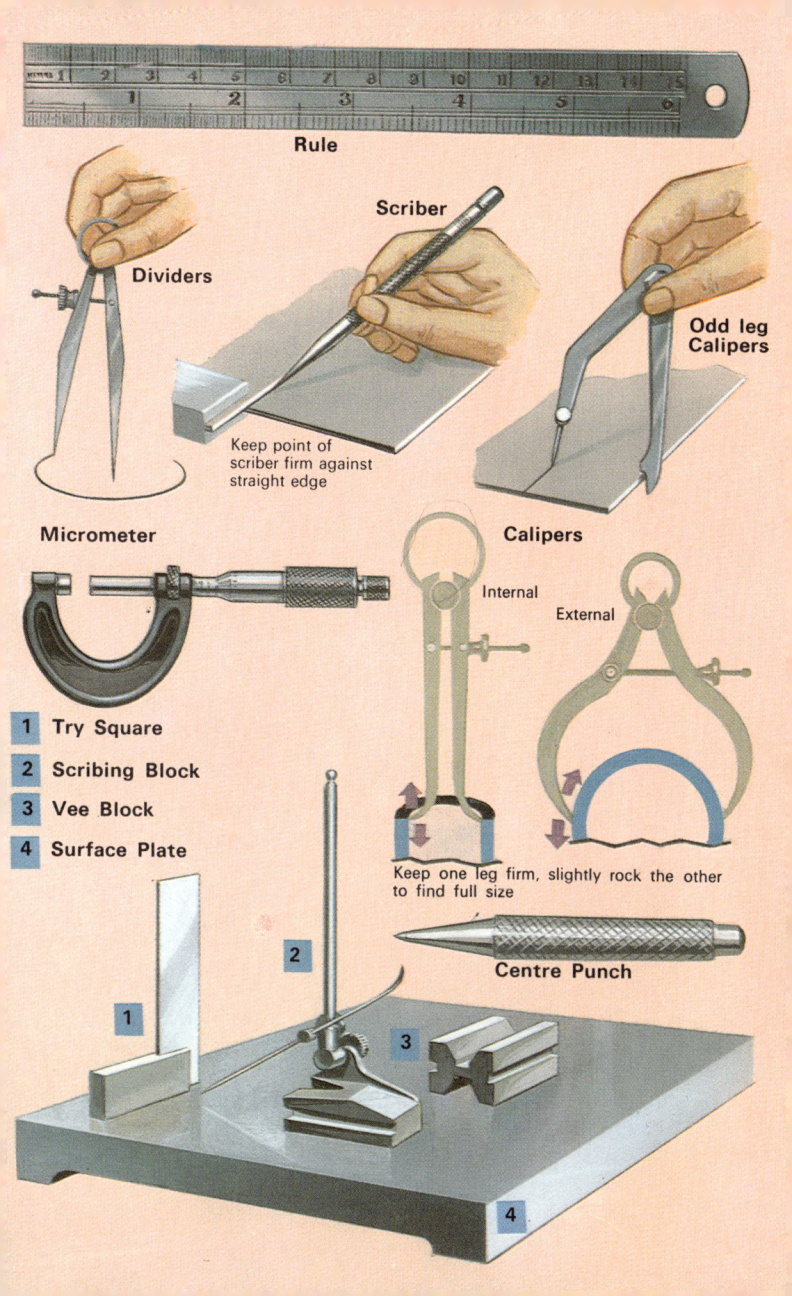

Dividers

Scriber

Keep point of scriber firm against straight edge

Odd leg Calipers

Micrometer

Calipers

Internal

External

Keep one leg firm, slightly rock the other to find full size

1 Try Square
2 Scribing Block
3 Vee Block
4 Surface Plate

Centre Punch

Files and filing

The file is an essential tool used on almost every job. Files are made of cast steel, hardened and tempered on the blade but with the tang left soft. The tang fits into the wooden handle. Files are classified according to their size, cut and shape.

The *size* is the measurement of the blade only and can range from 3 to 20 inches (76mm – 508mm).

The *cut* is the number and size of the teeth, i.e. the coarseness. There are five main cuts: rough, bastard, second-cut, smooth and dead smooth.

The *shape* is the cross-section. The hand file has one edge without teeth; this is called the safe edge and it is especially useful for filing internal right-angled corners.

For very fine work *needle* or *Swiss* files are available in a large range of shapes.

File handles are usually of ash or beech. *It is highly dangerous to use a file without a handle.*

Accurate filing demands considerable skill. The work should always be held firmly in the vice, as low as possible and horizontal. A comfortable stance, with feet apart slightly to the left of the vice, is best. For cross-filing a long edge, the file is placed on the work at an angle and the stroke is made forwards and sideways simultaneously. The file must be kept horizontal throughout the stroke and downward pressure applied on the forward movement to make a cut. The return stroke is relaxed. Common errors are filing 'uphill' or 'downhill', or with a rocking motion which produces a rounded edge.

Drawfiling is a technique used to produce a fine filed surface. For this the file is gripped around the blade with both hands and balanced across the work. Drawing the file back and forth produces fine scratches all in one direction. For a highly polished surface emery cloth can be wrapped tightly round the blade and the drawfiling action continued.

USAGES

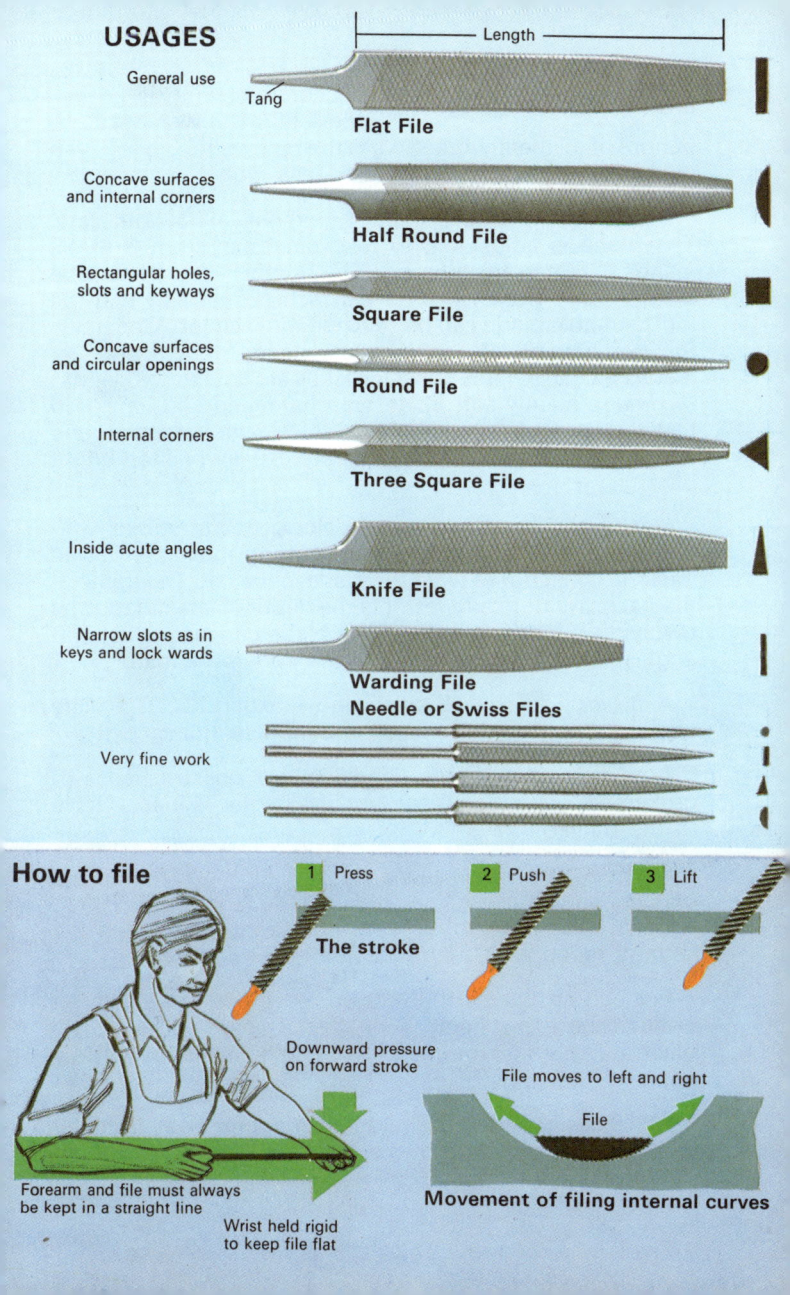

- **General use** — Flat File
- **Concave surfaces and internal corners** — Half Round File
- **Rectangular holes, slots and keyways** — Square File
- **Concave surfaces and circular openings** — Round File
- **Internal corners** — Three Square File
- **Inside acute angles** — Knife File
- **Narrow slots as in keys and lock wards** — Warding File
- **Very fine work** — Needle or Swiss Files

Length
Tang

How to file

The stroke
1. Press
2. Push
3. Lift

Forearm and file must always be kept in a straight line

Downward pressure on forward stroke

Wrist held rigid to keep file flat

Movement of filing internal curves
File moves to left and right
File

Saws and sawing

Accurate sawing is an important metalwork skill. A feature of all metalwork saws is the renewable blade; even with careful use they eventually wear out.

The *hacksaw* is the general purpose metalwork saw. The frame is adjustable to take blades of from 8 to 12 inches (203mm to 305mm). The number of teeth on the blades varies from 14 to 32 per inch (25mm) so that the most suitable blade can be selected for each job. Generally, thin and hard metals require a fine blade; for thick and soft metals a coarse blade is best. Blades are sold in two kinds: *flexible,* a mainly soft blade with hardened and tempered teeth, and *high speed steel,* which are hardened and tempered throughout. The latter are usually painted bright blue.

Hacksawing is done with a slow, steady stroke with pressure applied on the forward cutting movement. Care must be taken not to twist the blade in the cut. The frame of the hacksaw normally restricts the depth of the cut, but by revolving the adjusting pins the blade can be set at right angles to the frame, allowing deep cuts to be made.

A *junior hacksaw* is small and inexpensive. It is very useful for cutting thin metals and light sections.

A *padsaw* is a simple handle which utilises pieces of broken hacksaw blades for working in places inaccessible to the framed saw.

For fine sawing on jewellery and for silversmithing, a *piercing saw* is used. The blade is little more than $\frac{1}{16}$ inch wide (1·6mm), a simple wing-nut clamp holds it in the springy frame which supplies the necessary tension.

For cutting curves the *tension file* blade is used in an ordinary hacksaw frame with special adapting clips. The blade is like a fine round file and can be manoeuvred very easily.

All blades are fitted so that the teeth point away from the handle in the direction of the cut.

Saws and sawing

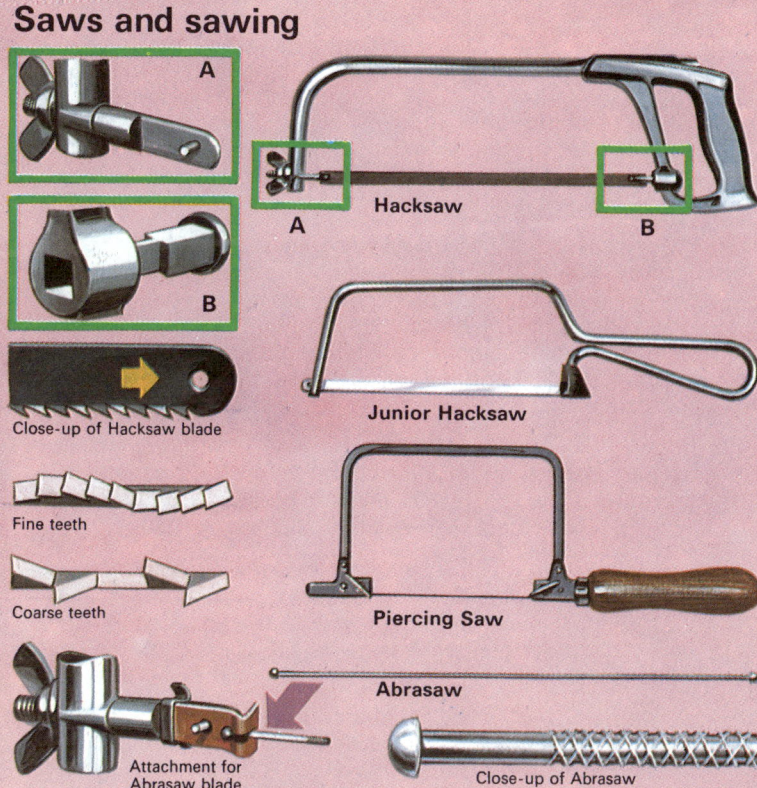

A

B

Hacksaw

A B

Close-up of Hacksaw blade

Fine teeth

Coarse teeth

Junior Hacksaw

Piercing Saw

Abrasaw

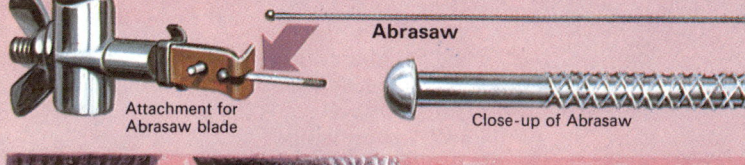

Attachment for Abrasaw blade

Close-up of Abrasaw

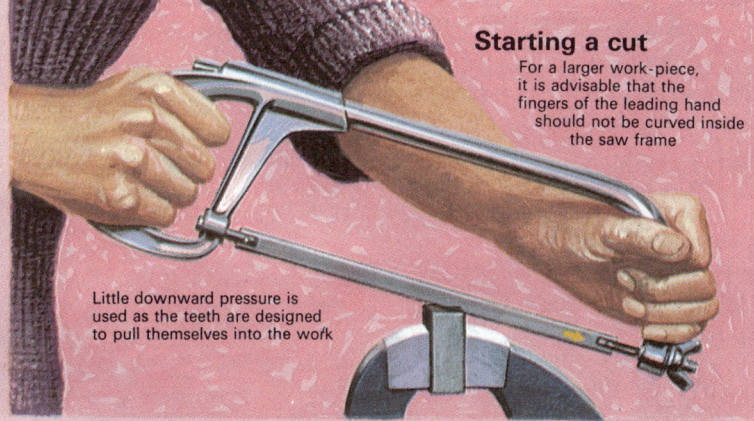

Starting a cut

For a larger work-piece, it is advisable that the fingers of the leading hand should not be curved inside the saw frame

Little downward pressure is used as the teeth are designed to pull themselves into the work

Drills and drilling

Most metalwork drilling is done with Morse twist drills which are available in many sizes. They are made of carbon steel (bright, shiny and fairly cheap) or high speed steel (black in colour and expensive). For power tools the latter drills are almost essential.

Twist drills have two cutting edges and the waste metal is lifted from the bottom of the drilling by the twin helical *flutes*. So that the body of the drill does not rub on the 'wall' of the hole, only a narrow strip called the *land* is the full nominal size. The *shank* of the drill is the part that fits into the drill chuck. On the larger sizes the shank is sometimes tapered so that it will lock into a tapered hole in the spindle of the drilling machine.

Drills become blunt after continual use and have to be reground. This operation takes skill but becomes easy with practice; beginners should seek expert help.

A sharp drill gives a clean cut and usually shavings are produced. A blunt drill will rub, squeak, become overheated with friction, eventually burn and be ruined. A sharp drill cuts well under gentle pressure (*the feed*) and should not be forced.

The speed of drills is important. Most large drilling machines have variable speeds which are changed by moving a belt on a series of pulleys. Charts show correct speeds, but a rule easy to remember is: *The bigger the drill the slower the speed.* Low speeds are also best on hard metals.

To reduce friction and overheating, cutting fluids are used, such as soluble oil on steels, and paraffin on aluminium.

There are several special drills, such as the countersink drill which opens out holes to take screw or rivet heads. Tank cutters and ring saws make large diameter holes in sheet metal.

Drilling on power machines can be dangerous. Concentration and obedience to safety rules is vital.

Morse Twist Drill

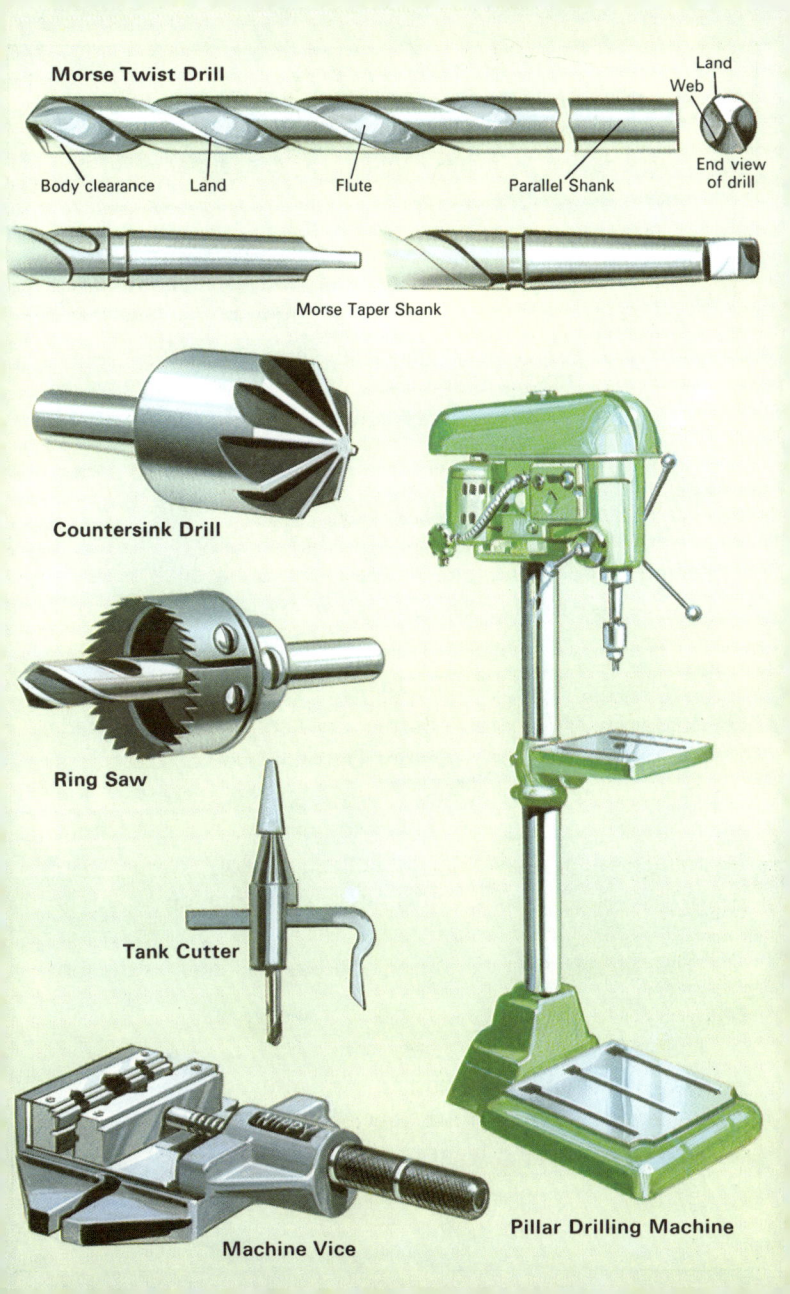

Body clearance — Land — Flute — Parallel Shank

Land
Web
End view of drill

Morse Taper Shank

Countersink Drill

Ring Saw

Tank Cutter

Machine Vice

Pillar Drilling Machine

Soft soldering

Soldering is a common way of joining metals. The process involves fusing a metal – solder – to the surfaces of the metals being joined.

All solders are alloys, i.e. mixtures of two or more metals. Soft solder is an alloy of tin and lead. This mixture, in various proportions, provides a range of solders for a variety of work; for example, tinman's solder for tinplate work has 50% tin and 50% lead. For electrical work solders are available which have a core of resin flux.

All soldering processes require heat. In soft soldering the heat comes from a soldering iron. The name 'iron' is misleading because the tip of the tool is copper, this metal being a good conductor of heat. Irons are available which are heated electrically; others can be heated over a gas flame.

In addition to solder and heat, a flux is essential in soldering. All metals discolour when they are heated. This is caused by oxidation. Once a layer of oxide has formed, the solder cannot fuse onto the surface of the metal. Fluxes help the solders to flow and act as a barrier to oxidation. Active fluxes actually dissolve oxides. An active flux for soft soldering is zinc chloride solution, sometimes called 'killed spirits'. Resin is a passive, barrier type, flux. The choice of iron and flux depends on the job in hand.

Sweat soldering involves coating both parts of the joint with solder and then bringing them into close contact and re-heating. Plumbers use specially prepared joints of this kind when joining lengths of copper pipe.

Soft Soldering

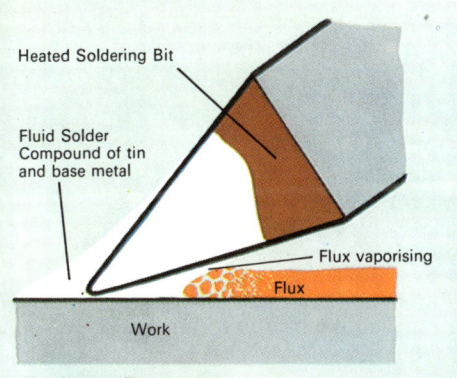

Heated Soldering Bit

Fluid Solder Compound of tin and base metal

Flux vaporising

Flux

Work

Soldering Process

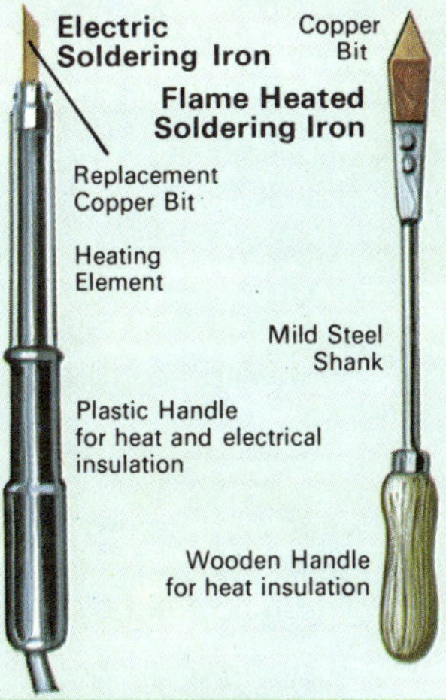

Electric Soldering Iron

Replacement Copper Bit

Heating Element

Plastic Handle for heat and electrical insulation

Flame Heated Soldering Iron

Copper Bit

Mild Steel Shank

Wooden Handle for heat insulation

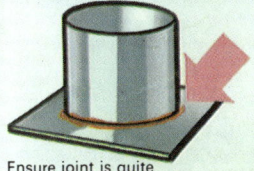

Ensure joint is quite clean - smear with flux

Heat iron in stove - when flame turns green iron is hot, but dirty

Clean iron with quick dip in liquid flux

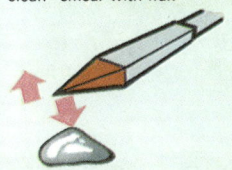

Apply to solder

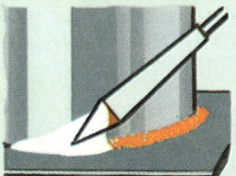

Move tip of iron slowly over join

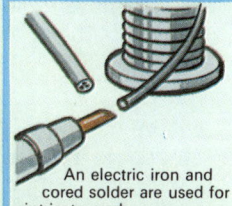

An electric iron and cored solder are used for intricate work

Sweat Soldering

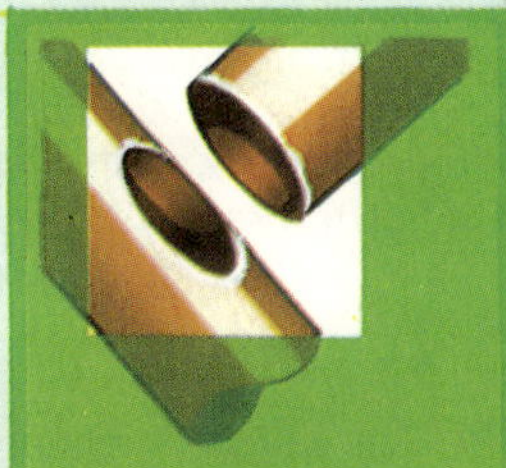

Coat both parts of joint with a layer of solder

Bring into close contact

Heat with bunsen or blowtorch flame

Hard soldering

Hard soldering gives a much stronger joint than soft soldering because the solders are harder and the melting temperatures higher.

There are two kinds of hard soldering – *brazing*, using a copper and zinc (brass) alloy as a solder, and *silver soldering*, using a silver/copper/zinc alloy.

In both methods a gas-burning brazing torch is used. The addition of blown air from a compressor produces a very hot flame. The flame is controlled by mixing the amounts of gas and air by the taps on the torch. A simple, firebrick-lined hearth supports the work.

The flux for hard soldering is mainly calcinated borax used as a powder or mixed into a paste with water. It prevents oxidation and helps the solder to flow. As with all soldering, the joint must be clean before work begins. Sometimes considerable ingenuity has to be used to hold the parts of the joint in close contact ready for soldering. A layer of flux is applied as a paste along the joint before heating starts. The brass solder – *spelter* – can be applied in one of two ways according to the job. (1) Lay small snippets of solder along the joint, this accurately controls the amount of solder used. (2) Bring the joint to red heat and then apply the spelter rod; this requires some skill.

Joints consisting of metals of different thicknesses must be heated so that the whole joint is brought to soldering temperature at the same moment. The glass-hard remains of the melted borax flux must be removed with great care.

Silver soldering is an identical process to brazing except that the metals being joined are usually non-ferrous with lower melting temperatures; care must be taken not to overheat them. Silver solders are available with a range of melting temperatures to enable complex constructions, such as teapots, to have a number of soldered joints close together.

Hard Soldering

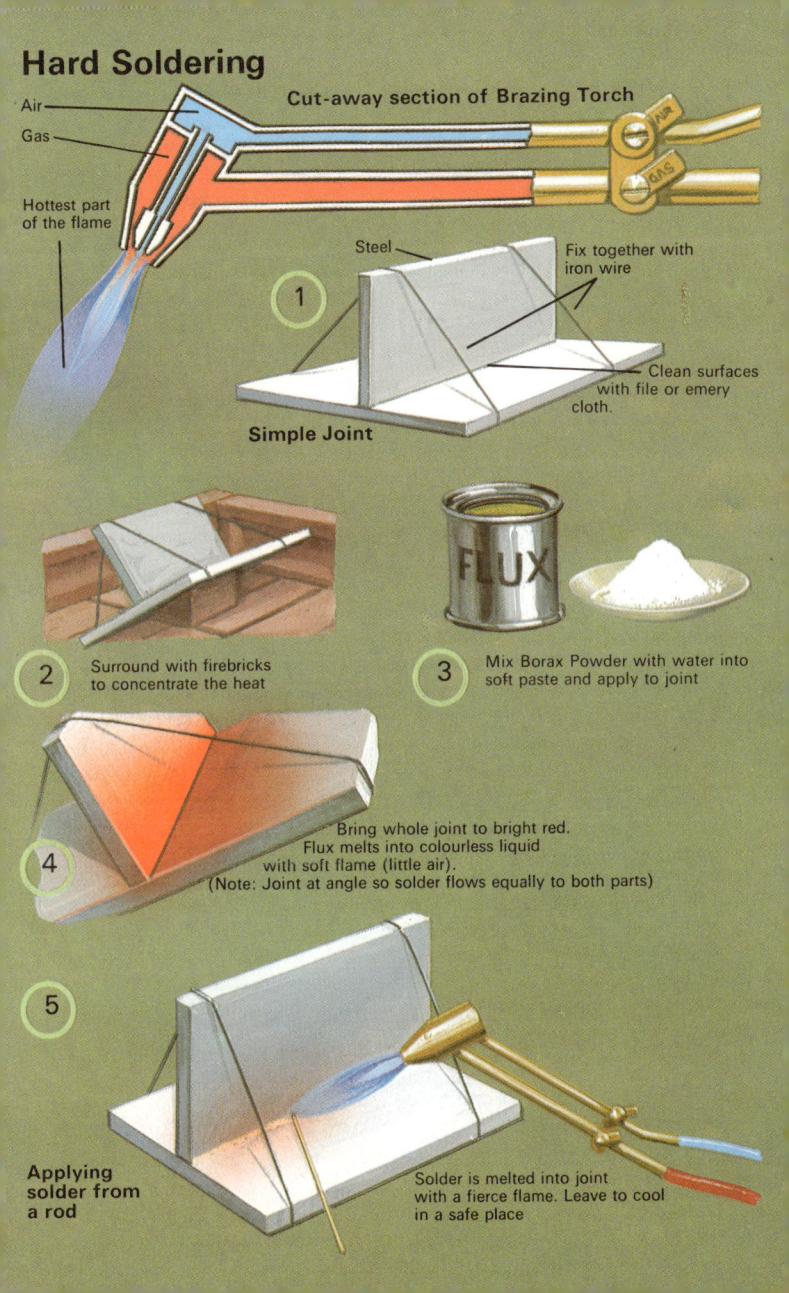

Cut-away section of Brazing Torch

- Air
- Gas
- Hottest part of the flame

1. Simple Joint
- Steel
- Fix together with iron wire
- Clean surfaces with file or emery cloth.

2.
Surround with firebricks to concentrate the heat

3.
Mix Borax Powder with water into soft paste and apply to joint

4.
Bring whole joint to bright red. Flux melts into colourless liquid with soft flame (little air).
(Note: Joint at angle so solder flows equally to both parts)

5. Applying solder from a rod
Solder is melted into joint with a fierce flame. Leave to cool in a safe place

External screw threads

Nuts, bolts and screws are made in a wide range of shapes, sizes and materials. (See front endpaper.) These fixings provide a means of joining materials together so that they can be taken apart later; parts of bicycles and motorcycles are good examples. Screw threads can also be cut on component parts to provide fixings.

External threads are cut on to metal rods using a *die* which is made of hardened and tempered cast steel. The die is held in a diestock by means of screws that can be adjusted to increase or decrease the cut of the die. The size stamped on the face of the die must equal the rod diameter, measured with calipers. Hitherto dies in Britain have been mainly in fractional imperial sizes, i.e. $\frac{3}{16}$", $\frac{1}{4}$", $\frac{3}{8}$", $\frac{1}{2}$", etc. Slowly changes are being made towards metric sizes, i.e. 6mm, 8mm, 10mm, etc. Both systems are likely to be used for the time being.

Screw threads are classified according to their profile, or shape; the many types include B.S.W. (British Standard Whitworth), B.S.F. (Fine) and B.A. (British Association). Gradually they are being replaced with a more uniform ISO metric system.

The clearance holes and the thread of the die are ground so that the die cuts best when the size and type markings are facing *downwards* onto the metal. Great care must be taken to start the thread true; the metal must be vertical in the vice and the die at right angles to its axis. Suitable lubricants help the cutting. The forwards and backwards action, shown in the illustration, allows the waste metal to break away and fall from the clearance holes. If the waste is allowed to clog the die it breaks off the crest of the thread and an inferior job results.

If the cut thread does not fit an internal thread, adjustments can be made with the grub screws and the thread re-cut.

Screw Threads (External)

Core or Root diameter

Nominal diameter or size

Root

Pitch

Crest

Grub Screws

Centre Screw

Circular Die

Die Stock

1 Bevel end of rod with file and select Die equal to rod diameter e.g. ¼" rod – ¼" Die

90°

Vice

2 Tighten Centre Screw

Fit Die into holder

3 Die face-down onto work

Check 90° and parallel

4 Lubricate with oil. Cut clockwise one turn. Half a turn back breaks away waste

5 Complete to required length

6 Sometimes threads will not mate. The remedy is to slacken centre screw, tighten grub screws and recut

Internal screw threads

Threads are cut into the 'wall' of a hole with a tap. The process is called *tapping*. Taps are made of hardened and tempered cast steel and high speed steel. The *taper* tap is tapered for almost half its length; this enables it to get started and begin to cut. The *second cut* has a smaller taper. The final cut is made with a *plug* tap; this has hardly any taper and is especially useful for finishing threads to the bottom of 'blind' holes (i.e. holes that do not go right through the metal). It is sometimes called a *bottoming* tap for this reason.

The size and type of tap is selected to match exactly that of the die or bolt to be used.

A suitable hole must first be drilled. This stage often confuses beginners. The *tapping size* hole must be *smaller* than the size marked on the tap to allow the thread to be cut into the 'wall' of the hole (see diagram). The tapping size hole for each size of tap can be found in tables.

The square shank at the end of the tap fits into the *tap wrench*. The cutting action is the same forward and backward movement used with a die. The forward movement cuts the thread; the backward movement breaks away the waste metal which falls down the *flutes* along the length of the tap.

Tapping 'blind' holes calls for great care; the waste metal collects at the bottom of the hole and can cause the tap to jam tight. Because cast steel is very brittle, taps can easily snap off inside the work: this causes, at best, a delay and, at worst, a ruined job. For this reason the waste should be knocked out of the hole periodically. Lubrication also helps.

Very great care must be taken to start the tap vertically to the axis of the hole by using an engineer's square; otherwise a distorted thread will result.

Screw Threads

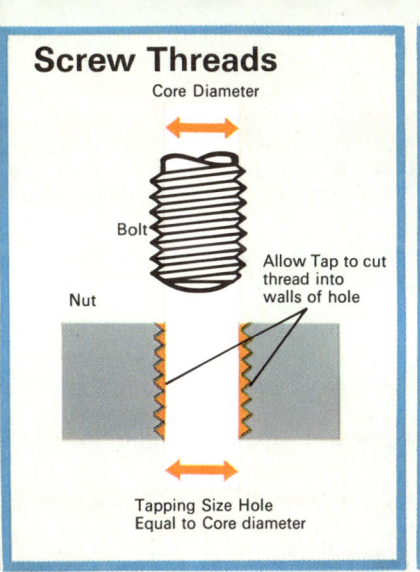

Core Diameter

Bolt

Nut

Allow Tap to cut thread into walls of hole

Tapping Size Hole Equal to Core diameter

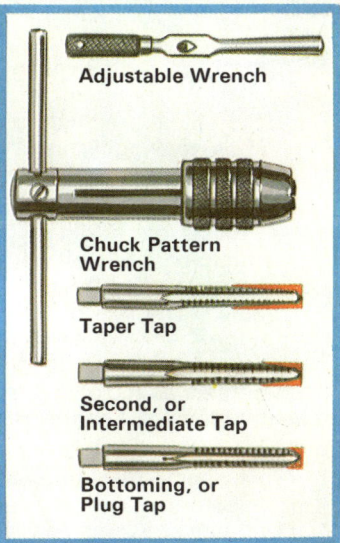

Adjustable Wrench

Chuck Pattern Wrench

Taper Tap

Second, or Intermediate Tap

Bottoming, or Plug Tap

1 Find out tapping size by consulting chart or table. Drill the hole

2 Fix job in vice so that hole is vertical (90°)

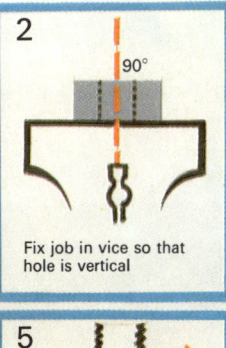

3 Select correct Tap. This must match rod diameter, and die size and type

4 Use Taper Tap to get started

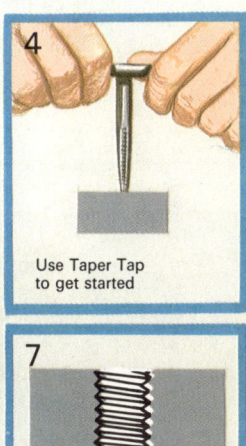

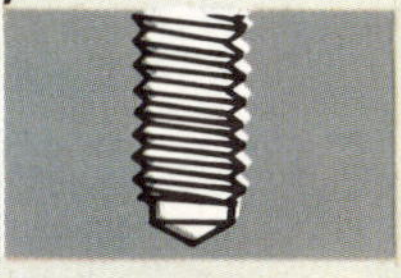

5 Apply cutting fluid

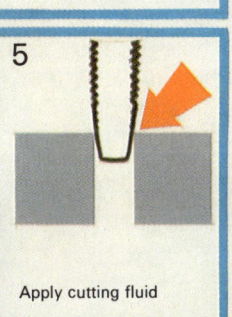

6 Turn Wrench clockwise to cut . . . . . . and then back to clear swarf

7 A blind-hole is tapped by using all 3 Taps in turn, starting with the Taper Tap

Riveting

Riveting is a simple but effective way of joining metals. It is used extensively in shipbuilding, aircraft construction, civil engineering, etc. Often riveting is used when a simple movable joint is required; a pair of tongs is an example.

Rivets are available in several metals — copper, brass, aluminium and soft iron being the most common. Usually the material of the rivet should match the materials being joined. The size of the rivet is measured by the diameter of the shank. For each size, rivets are available in a variety of lengths. The shape of the rivet head is an important feature and must be selected to suit the job. For example, a countersunk head rivet allows a flush surface finish.

A special rivet, originally developed for use in the aircraft industry but now available to the home craftsman, is the *'pop'* rivet. As the central pin is withdrawn, using a special tool, the end of the rivet deforms and the plates of the joint are squeezed together. When the strain on the pin becomes too great it fractures with a 'pop' at the thinned neck. The pop rivet can be especially useful where the joint is accessible only from one side.

To close a snap-headed rivet, a simple tool called a *snap* is used to support the hemispherical head of the rivet. Riveting calls for the skilful use of the hammer, and this is why the metalworker's hammer has a ball pein head.

Careful alignment of the holes in each plate is important. Whenever possible, all the holes are drilled in one plate first. Then *one* matching hole is drilled in the second plate; a rivet is inserted and closed. Using the holes in the top plate as a guide, the drilling of the other holes in the second plate is completed.

To obtain a movable joint, paper or card is placed between the two parts; the rivet is closed and then the paper or card is burnt away.

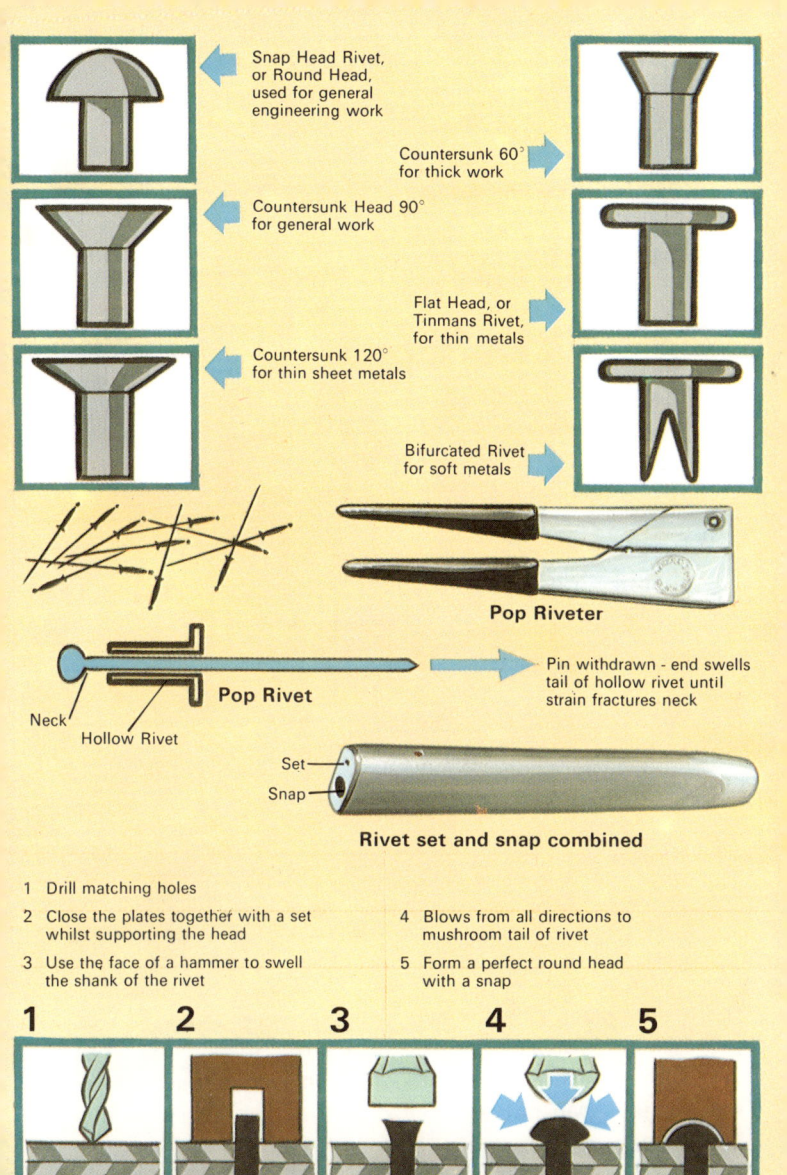

Snap Head Rivet, or Round Head, used for general engineering work

Countersunk 60° for thick work

Countersunk Head 90° for general work

Flat Head, or Tinmans Rivet, for thin metals

Countersunk 120° for thin sheet metals

Bifurcated Rivet for soft metals

Pop Riveter

Pop Rivet

Neck Hollow Rivet

Pin withdrawn - end swells tail of hollow rivet until strain fractures neck

Set
Snap

Rivet set and snap combined

1. Drill matching holes
2. Close the plates together with a set whilst supporting the head
3. Use the face of a hammer to swell the shank of the rivet
4. Blows from all directions to mushroom tail of rivet
5. Form a perfect round head with a snap

1 **2** **3** **4** **5**

Sheet metalwork

Highly complex sheet metal shapes, such as car body parts, are mass-produced rapidly using giant presses. Simpler work can be produced by carefully cutting shapes out of sheet material, then bending and folding them to make a three-dimensional form. The shape, which is marked out on the sheet metal, is called the *development.*

Extra metal is allowed on the development for strengthening the edges and for overlaps to form the riveted or spot-welded joints. Bending lines are also carefully marked. Sometimes the order in which the bends and folds have to be made is important and requires careful thought before the work begins.

The edges of thin sheets can be sharp and dangerous; they are stiffened and made safe either by folding over the edge or by rolling the edge over a stout wire. Sheets can be joined together by overlapping and then soldering or riveting, or by folding and hooking the edges together to form a seam. Joints like these can be seen on food cans.

Sheet metalworking tools are very simple. The sheet is cut by bench shears or hand snips according to the size of the job. The cuts must be made accurately. The developed sheets are bent with soft mallets of hide, plastic or rubber. Metal hammers would dent and damage the metal. Only when working tight bends, as in making a wired edge, are special panning hammers used.

Any piece of metal over which another piece of metal is formed is called a *stake.* The sheet metalworker has a wide range of stakes, some of which have strange-sounding names – pan-bottom, half moon, hatchet, three-arm and funnel – are just a few.

Development

Allowance for making wire edge

Front

B B
A A

Side Bottom Side

B B
A A

Back

Green dotted line indicates fold

A to be riveted to B

Straight Tinsnips

Curved Tinsnips

Universal Pattern

Panning Hammer

Boxwood Mallet

Soft-Faced Bossing Mallet

1 Mark off the lap

2 Close down

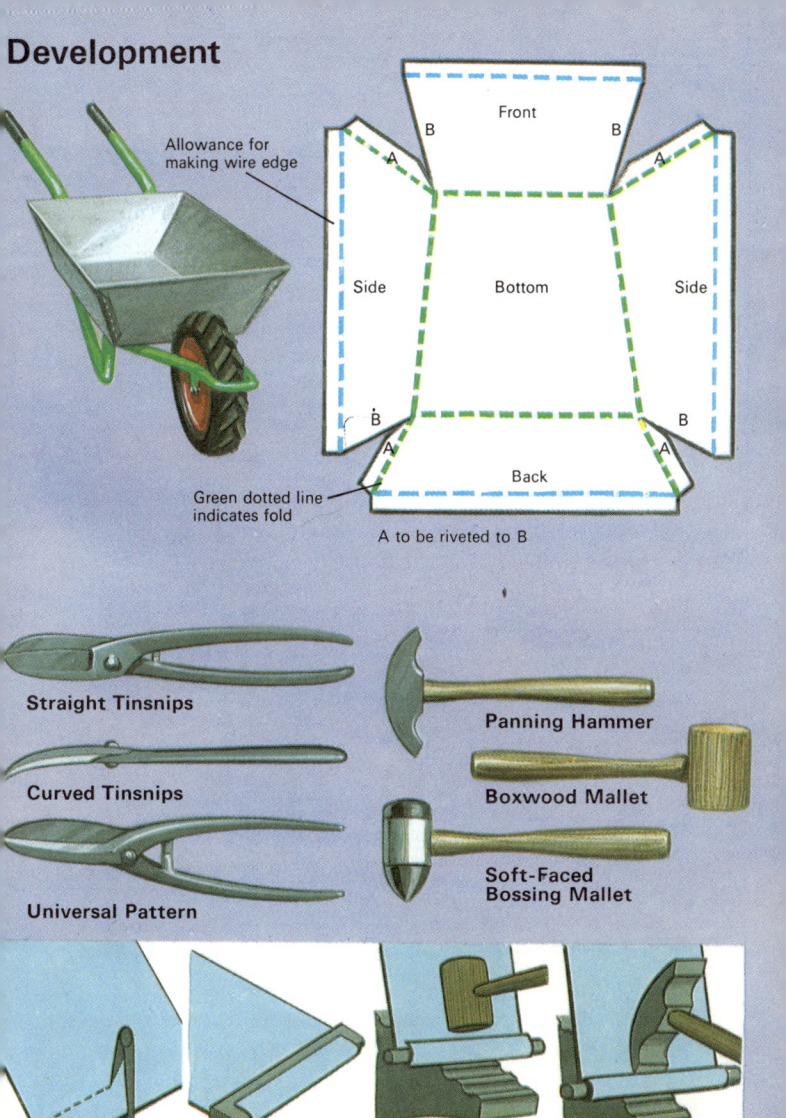

3 Insert Wire and turn edge over on a Creasing Iron

4 Tuck in edge

Making a Wire Edge

Forging 1
Tools and equipment

When ferrous metals are hot they are much easier to bend, twist and stretch. Working hot metals is called forging – the craft of the blacksmith.

The smith's materials are iron and steel and his essential equipment is his fire, or forge. The forge hearth is of sheet steel lined with firebricks. A wide hood directs the smoke and fumes to the flue. The fuel is small coke. To increase the heat of the fire a forced draught of air is provided by an electric fan. The air enters the back of the forge through a cast iron tube called a tuyere, which is kept cool by a water jacket. It is at the end of the tuyere that waste, called clinker, forms after combustion.

A good clean fire is essential, and it is important to warm up fresh coke on the fringes of the fire and dry it completely before raking it to the centre of the fire.

The smith's *anvil* is of wrought iron with a hard cast steel face. It usually weighs about one cwt (51kg). The face has a square *hardie hole* designed to hold a variety of special tools. It also has a round hole for punching, a small area of soft metal for cutting on with *sets*, and a beak, or bick, which gives a variety of curves and arcs.

Tongs have many different mouth shapes. Tightly gripping tongs make for safe work.

The smith has a large selection of special tools for shaping and forming. *Swages* for making round sections, *punches* for making holes, *sets* for cutting and *fullers* for quickly reducing work ready for flattening with *flatters*. Most of these tools have a top half which has a handle and a bottom half which is a tapered square shank to fit the hardie hole in the anvil. A helper acts as a *striker*, usually with a sledge hammer.

Forging

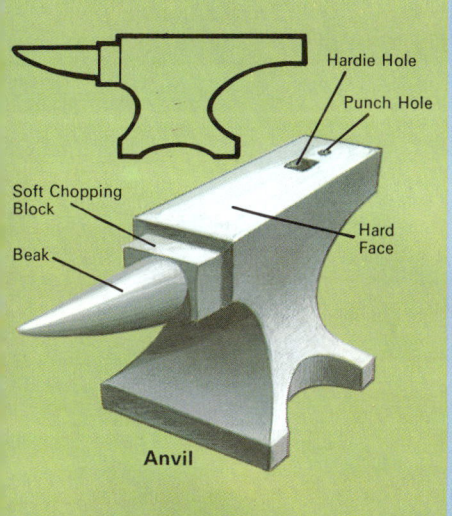

Anvil
- Hardie Hole
- Punch Hole
- Soft Chopping Block
- Hard Face
- Beak

Hollow Bit Tongs

Pick Up, or Dandy, Tongs

Open Mouth Tongs

Closed Mouth Tongs

Swage for producing round sections

Flatter for smoothing a rough surface

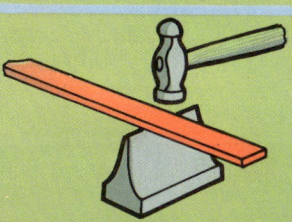

Hardie for cutting hot metals

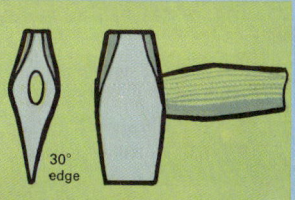

Hot Set for cutting hot bars
- 30° edge

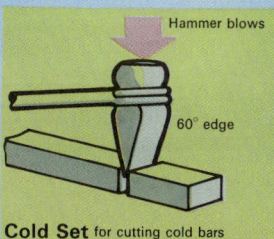

Cold Set for cutting cold bars
- Hammer blows
- 60° edge

Forging 2

'Strike while the iron is hot' is a well-known saying. It is fundamental to successful forgework because wrought iron and mild steel are at their most ductile and malleable when at red heat. The forge is usually fitted in a shaded part of a workshop so that the heat colour can be seen more easily. With a very hot fire, beginners can easily make the mistake of allowing the metal to burn away – usually in a spectacular shower of sparks.

Once the metal reaches red heat, speed is essential. All the necessary tools should be at hand and the anvil within easy reach. For safety a leather apron should be worn and often thick leather gloves are useful.

Drawing down lengthens and reduces the metal and can be used to change the section – a square tapered point on the end of a rod for example. *Spreading* is similar to drawing down but the hammering is confined to the two opposite faces, allowing the metal to spread sideways as it thins out. The first stages of forming a screwdriver blade include spreading.

Upsetting, or *jumping-up*, increases the cross-section of the metal by causing it to bulge. This is often used as a preliminary to bending right angles in bars, during which the metal tends to thin.

Cutting with sets or hardie. This is done for speed since it is much faster than hacksawing. The bar is nicked from both sides with the sets and then snapped off with a smart hammer blow over the edge of the anvil.

Twisting is used as a decorative feature on much iron work. Provided the metal is evenly heated it is simple to do and excellently illustrates the ductility of hot metals.

Scrolls are decorative features used in gates, fences and screens. They can be formed over the beak of the anvil or, more usually, on a scrolling tool held in a vice.

Forging an eye

A Calculate length (π × diameter) and mark with a Dot Punch

B Bend to a right angle

C Turn over end

D Continue turning

E Close the loop

Drawing down
a square point

1. Heat metal to red heat – forge a short sharp point

2. Reheat metal. Hammer at base of point to lengthen

Anvil face

3. Continue forging point to required length. Leave work to cool slowly

section of metal

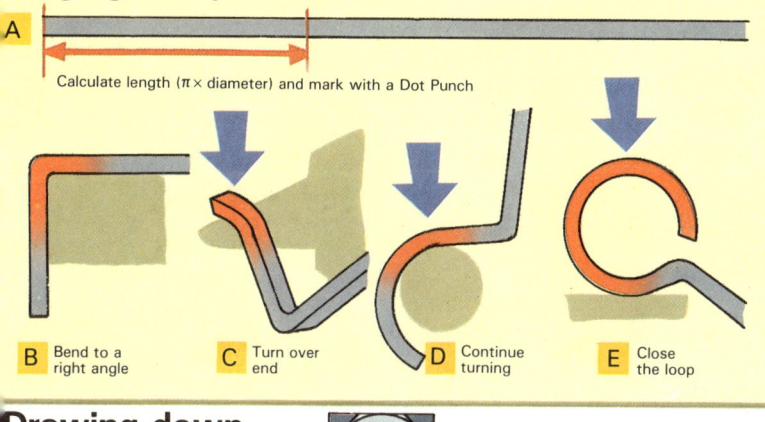

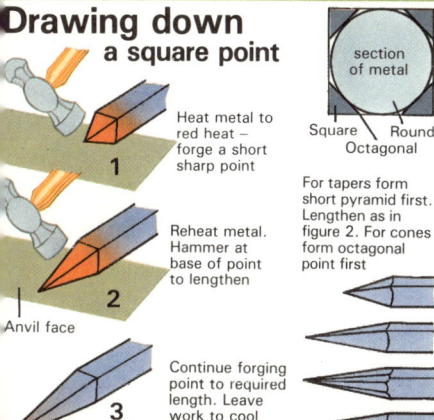

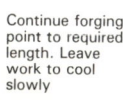

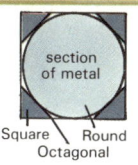

Square — Round
Octagonal

For tapers form short pyramid first. Lengthen as in figure 2. For cones form octagonal point first

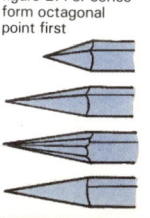

a round point

Proceed as in figures 1 and 2. Reheat the metal. Hammer the corners to form an octagonal point

4. Reheat the metal. Hammer all corners until a round point of the right length is formed

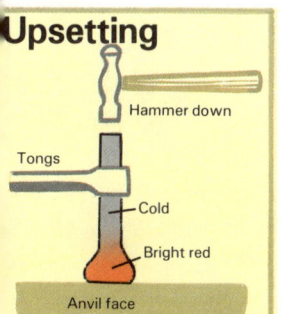

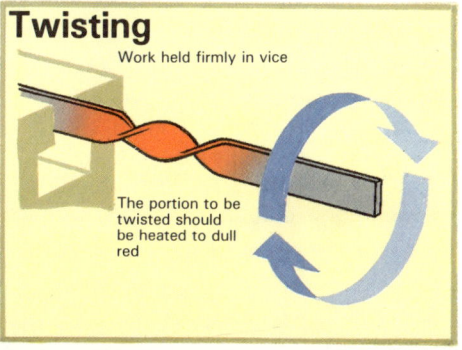

5. Leave the work to cool slowly on the hearth

Upsetting

Hammer down

Tongs

Cold

Bright red

Anvil face

Twisting

Work held firmly in vice

The portion to be twisted should be heated to dull red

Heat treatment 1
Hardening and tempering

Metals can be made softer or harder by heat treatments. Basically these involve heating the metal to a certain critical temperature and then controlling the speed at which it cools. In this way saw blades, chisels, drills, etc., are made hard and tough enough to cut other metals. Metals can also be made soft and pliable so that they can be easily shaped.

After heat treatment the appearance of the metal is little changed but changes have taken place within its structure. In simple terms, the heating causes the particles of the metal to move around; the cooling process fixes the particles into new arrangements. Heat treatments can vary considerably from one metal to another. For example, heating red hot and quenching in water will harden steel but soften copper.

Hardening and tempering. A large number of tools are made of steel containing about 0.8% carbon. This steel can be made very tough by a simple process. First the work is *hardened;* it is brought to cherry-red heat with a brazing torch flame and then quickly quenched in tepid water – cold water cools too quickly and can crack the metal.

After hardening, the metal is extremely hard and very brittle. To bring it to maximum hardness with minimum brittleness it has to be *tempered.* The work is cleaned of surface oxides and then very gently re-heated over a bunsen burner or in a simple muffle made of a length of steel tube. Very soon oxide colours begin to appear on the bright surface.

These colours give a very accurate indication of temperature. When the correct colour reaches the tip or the cutting edge of the tool it is again quenched. A careful look at the ends of a hacksaw blade will reveal signs of the tempering colours.

Hardening and Tempering

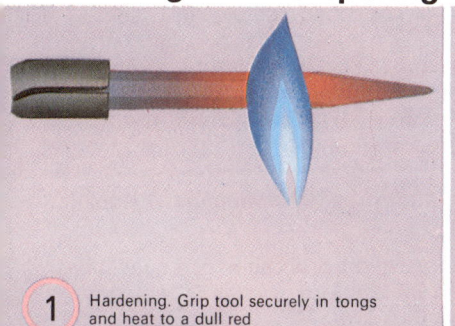

1. Hardening. Grip tool securely in tongs and heat to a dull red 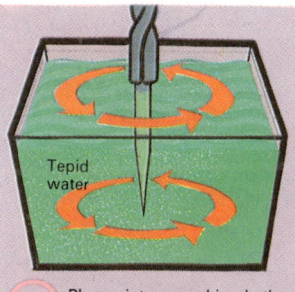
2. Plunge into quenching bath and keep tool moving in circular direction 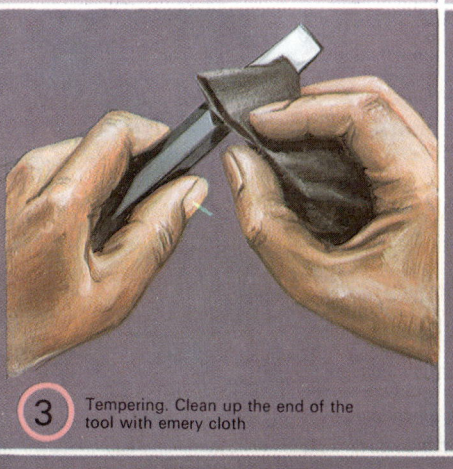
3. Tempering. Clean up the end of the tool with emery cloth 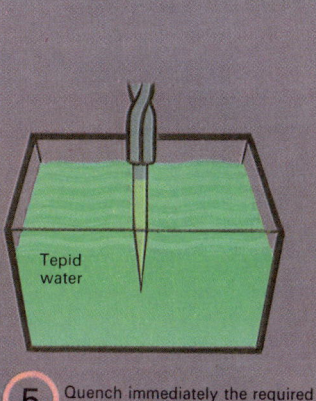
4. Re-heat
5. Quench immediately the required colour develops

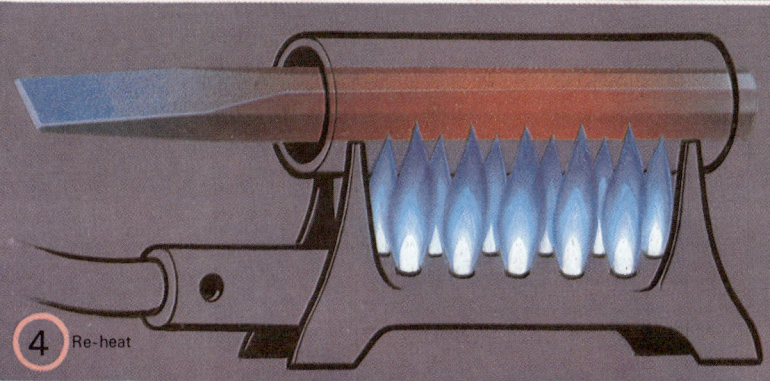

Heat treatment 2
Annealing

When metals are hammered and bent they become hard. This is known as *work-hardening*. Most people know how easy it is to break a metal paper clip or piece of wire by bending it back and forth a few times. Work hardening is caused by the stresses being set up within the metal; these stresses can be relieved by a heat treatment called *annealing*. Annealing softens metals.

Each metal has an annealing process which suits it best. Here are the processes for the most common metals:

Copper is heated to a dull red with a gentle brazing or bunsen flame, then quenched in water. This leaves the copper soft but badly discoloured with surface oxides. These black and purple marks can be removed by dipping the copper into a 'pickle' bath of dilute sulphuric acid (1 part of acid to 10 parts of water) holding the work with brass or copper tongs. A light scrubbing with pumice powder following a water wash results in a dull pink finish.

Brass is annealed like copper but allowed to cool in air and not quenched.

Aluminium shows very little colour change in the early stages of heating. It has a very low melting temperature and is easy to overheat. To overcome these problems the aluminium is marked with soap before heating; when the soap mark turns black or dark brown the correct annealing temperature has been reached. Cool in the air.

Zinc is annealed by immersing it in boiling water.

Steels are heated to bright red and left to cool very slowly in a safe place. The cooling process can be prolonged by covering the work with hot coke.

It is useful to remember that in operations such as soldering and forging, heat treatments may take place incidentally. Thus a forged piece of mild steel is best left to cool slowly and become annealed if it is to be filed or drilled later.

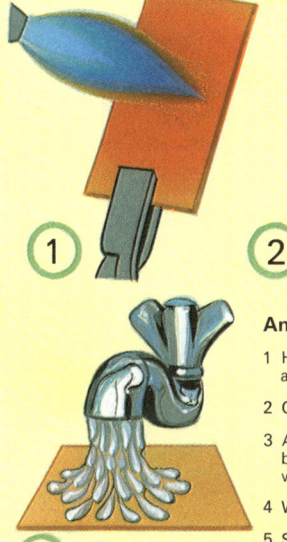

Annealing Copper

1. Heat copper to dull red using a Brazing Torch
2. Cool by quenching in water
3. Acid Bath. Brass tongs should be used in the acid as steel will contaminate the solution
4. Wash clean with water
5. Scrub with pumice powder

Annealing Aluminium

1. Use soap to mark as temperature indicator
2. When soap turns black the metal is annealed

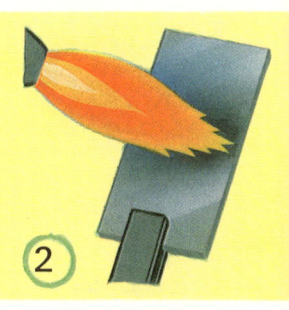

Annealing Steel

1. Heat to bright red
2. Allow to cool slowly in a safe place

Beaten metalwork

When malleable, non-ferrous sheet metals are beaten with special hammers onto steel stakes, they stretch and deform. The skill of the silversmith is in controlling these changes in shape. Dishes, bowls, cups, jugs and teapots are produced in this way.

Hollowing is the first stage in producing shallow shapes. The annealed metal blank is beaten down into a hollow in a wooden block, or onto a leather sandbag, with a domed *bossing mallet.* Sometimes a round-end *blocking hammer* is used. The blank is held at an angle to the hollow; starting from the edge it is slowly revolved and beaten down into the hollow, gradually working towards the centre.

Hollowing gives only a roughly shaped dish. To true the work to an accurate profile, and to *work-harden* it, a process called *planishing* follows. For planishing, slightly convex-faced hammers are used, together with a convex-faced stake. Both hammer and stake are highly polished, as marks on either will be transferred to the work. To guide the hammer blows, concentric circles are drawn with a pencil compass on the underside of the dish. The dish is held onto the stake by its edge. This time the hammer blows are directed at the centre first and, as the dish is slowly revolved, the blows spiral outwards to the edge. Great skill is needed to make each hammer mark overlap the last, and each *course*, or row, overlap the one before so that the whole surface is systematically covered. The hammer blows should be fairly light, of even weight, and delivered from a range of a few inches only.

Planishing leaves the surface covered with small hammer marks. This finish is a by-product of the process and can be removed if desired.

Forms that are basically cylindrical or conical – vases and beakers for example – are developed on flat sheets and then rolled and seamed by silver soldering along the edge-to-edge butt joint. These shapes are trued and finished by planishing.

Hollowing

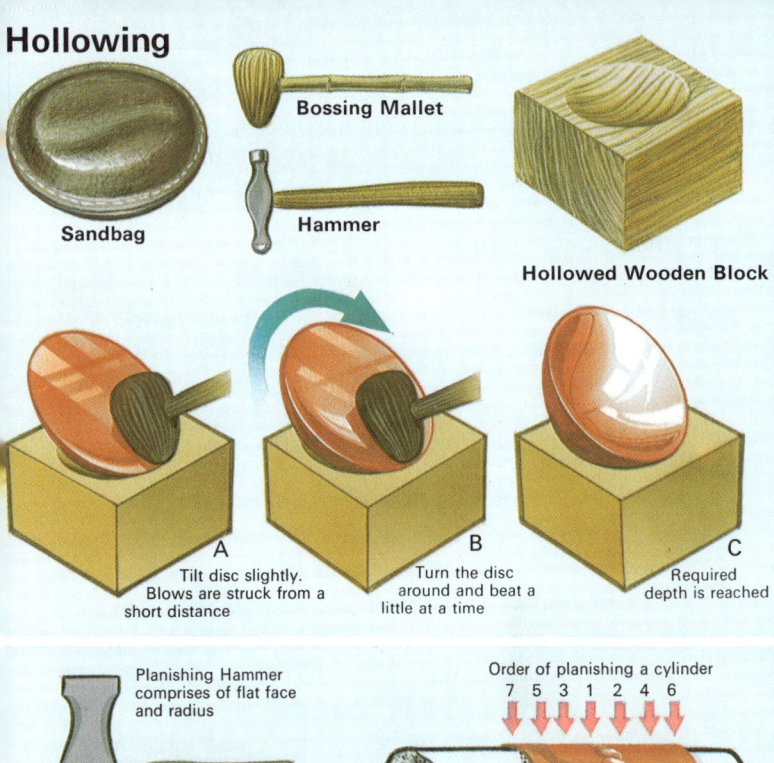

Sandbag

Bossing Mallet

Hammer

Hollowed Wooden Block

A Tilt disc slightly. Blows are struck from a short distance

B Turn the disc around and beat a little at a time

C Required depth is reached

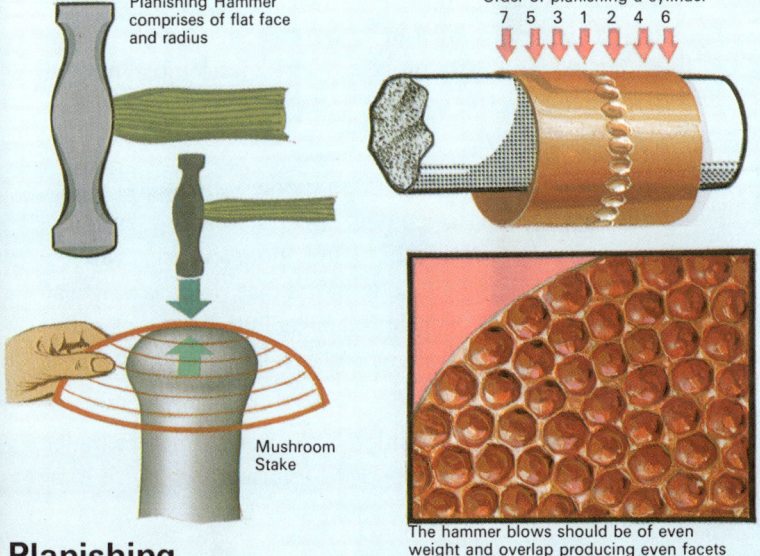

Planishing Hammer comprises of flat face and radius

Mushroom Stake

Order of planishing a cylinder
7 5 3 1 2 4 6

The hammer blows should be of even weight and overlap producing even facets

Planishing

Beaten metalwork

Deep bowls and tall forms, such as vases and the bodies of coffee pots, can be made from a single blank of metal without jointing, by using a process called *raising*.

The size of the blank required is first carefully calculated from accurate full-size drawings. The non-ferrous blank of silver, gilding metal or copper is annealed to soften it, carefully cleaned and then marked with concentric circles using a pencil compass. These pencil lines act as a guide for each *course*, or row, of hammer blows and help to ensure that the form 'grows' evenly.

In raising, the disc is beaten from the outside, working from the centre and forcing the metal towards the edge. The work is held up to the stake at an angle and the mallet or hammer blows strike the metal in advance of the edge of the stake, pushing it downwards. After each blow the work is revolved slightly so that each blow just overlaps the last. The hammer blows must be of equal weight and a rhythmic beating pattern helps. The metal must not be trapped between the hammer and the stake as this would cause it to thin out.

After a few courses have been worked, the metal needs to be re-annealed to combat work-hardening stresses. After annealing and cleaning up, more courses can be raised. Gradually the diameter of the disc decreases whilst the depth increases. Raising is usually followed by planishing to true-up the final shape and to remove any tool marks left by the raising hammer.

When a small, upstand edge is required, a much simpler raising process, shown opposite, is used.

Raising

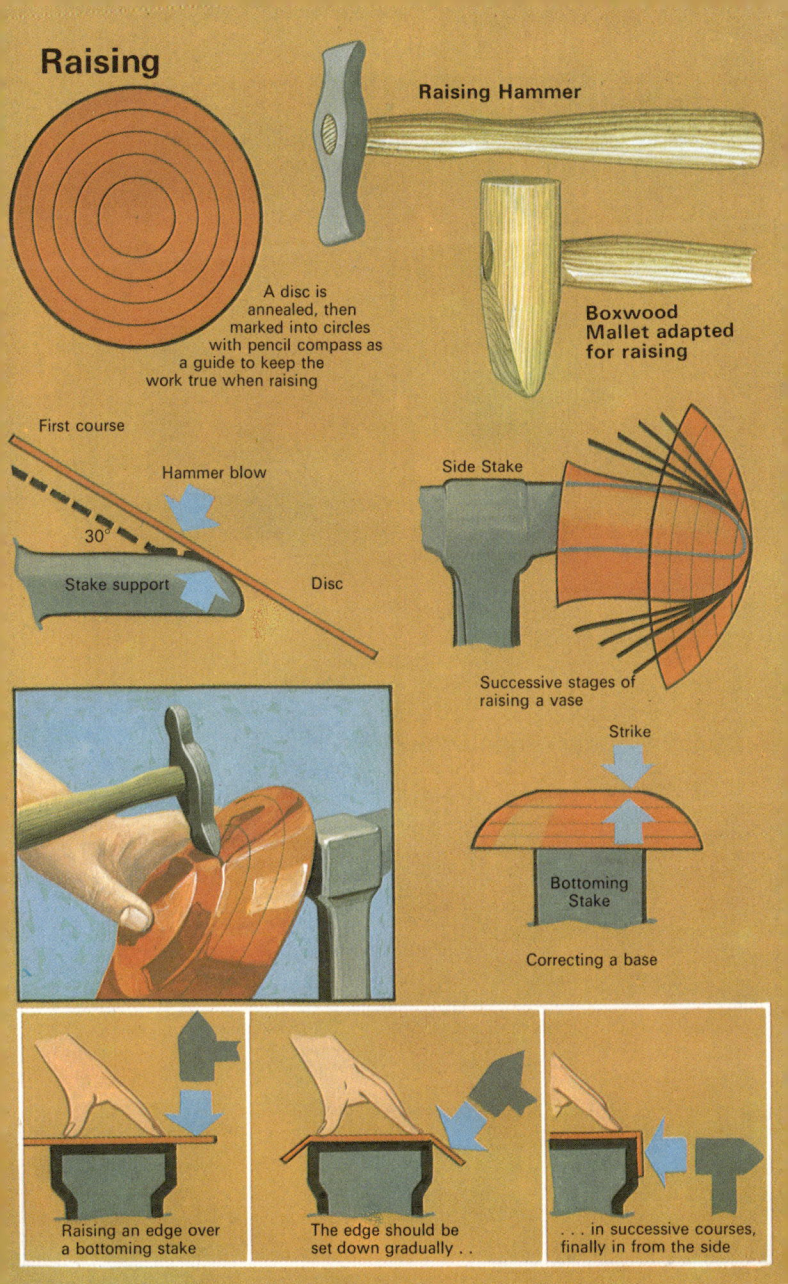

A disc is annealed, then marked into circles with pencil compass as a guide to keep the work true when raising

Raising Hammer

Boxwood Mallet adapted for raising

First course
Hammer blow
30°
Stake support
Disc

Side Stake

Successive stages of raising a vase

Strike
Bottoming Stake

Correcting a base

Raising an edge over a bottoming stake

The edge should be set down gradually . .

. . . in successive courses, finally in from the side

Casting — foundrywork

Complex metal shapes, like car engine parts and water taps, would be almost impossible to produce by sawing, drilling and filing methods. Early Man quickly discovered that metal, when very hot, became molten, behaved like a liquid, and as it cooled became solid again. Early spear and axe heads were produced in this way. The process is called casting.

The skilled craftsman in foundry work is the *patternmaker*. He makes the wooden pattern from which the cavity in sand is formed later to receive the molten metal. The pattern is carefully designed with slightly rounded corners and slightly tapered sides so that it can be withdrawn easily from the sand.

The moulding sand contains some clay. This binds the particles together and gives a sharp reproduction of the pattern. Some sands are oil-mixed and ready to use; others have to be carefully mixed with water until the right consistency is found.

The drawings show the sequence of operations. Great care must be taken at each stage and the order of operations is very important. The metals for casting are prepared in a furnace heated by gas, oil or coke, and usually have a forced air blast from a compressor to increase the heat of the flame. The metal is melted in a crucible made of plumbago – a mixture of graphite and fireclay. The ingots of metal are fed in when the crucible becomes red hot and are heated until they become liquid.

Each metal has an ideal temperature at which it can be poured into the mould; a *pyrometer* is used to check the temperature of the melt.

The crucible with its molten metal is removed from the furnace with special lifting tongs and is placed in a long-handled ring shank; two people pour the metal into the mould. This is obviously a very dangerous stage and requires very strict safety precautions.

Casting

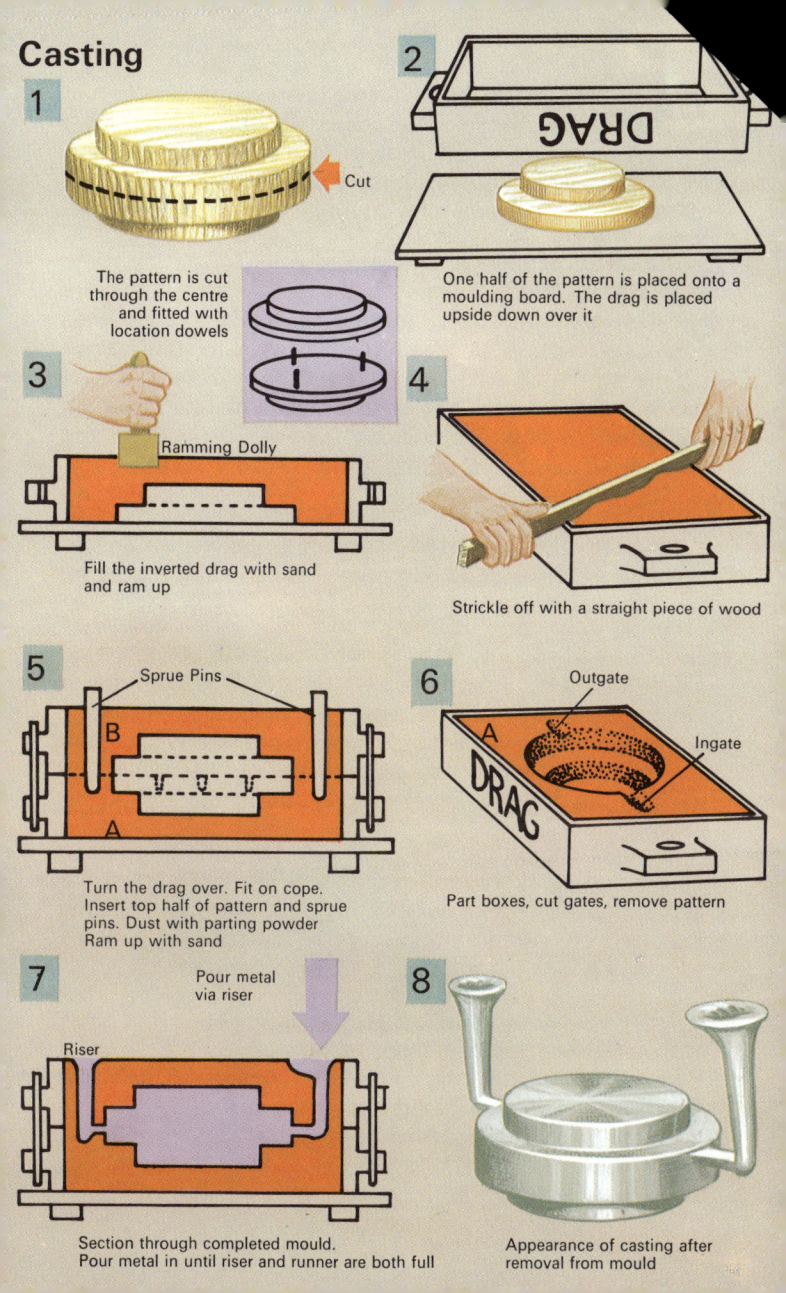

1. The pattern is cut through the centre and fitted with location dowels

2. One half of the pattern is placed onto a moulding board. The drag is placed upside down over it

3. Ramming Dolly — Fill the inverted drag with sand and ram up

4. Strickle off with a straight piece of wood

5. Sprue Pins — Turn the drag over. Fit on cope. Insert top half of pattern and sprue pins. Dust with parting powder. Ram up with sand

6. Outgate — Ingate — Part boxes, cut gates, remove pattern

7. Pour metal via riser — Riser — Section through completed mould. Pour metal in until riser and runner are both full

8. Appearance of casting after removal from mould

The lathe

The modern lathe is a development of one of the earliest machine tools. It has played an important part in the growth of modern industry and mass-production. Today lathes can be completely automated and require minimum attention from their operators.

The basic principle is simple. The work is fixed by some means to a spindle driven by an electric motor. As the metal revolves at speed, cutting tools are brought into contact with it and the waste is cut away. If the tool travels parallel to the spindle axis cylindrical forms are made. If the tool cuts at right angles to the axis, flat surfaces are produced. At any tool position between $0° - 90°$ to the axis, tapers or conical forms result.

Drilling, boring, making threads, knurling and screw-cutting are other operations that can be carried out on this versatile machine, producing work of very high precision.

Lathe tools are usually made of high-speed steel (H.S.S.) and are ground to various shapes to cover a wide range of work. Round-nosed tools give a fine finish whilst knife tools are necessary to work sharp corners. Grinding lathe tools demands great care and skill since the angles – top rake and clearance – have to be correct for each of the different kinds of metal being turned.

For efficient cutting, the cutting edge of the tool has to be aligned carefully with the axis of the work up to the centre line. To reduce overheating and tool wear coolants are often used when turning. Water and soluble oil mixed to a milky-looking solution is commonly used.

There are various ways of setting up the lathe. For short work and *facing-off*, a three or four-jaw chuck is used. Parallel turning on long lengths is carried out *between centres*, the material being supported at both ends. For holding irregular shaped work, a *face plate* is used.

Lathe

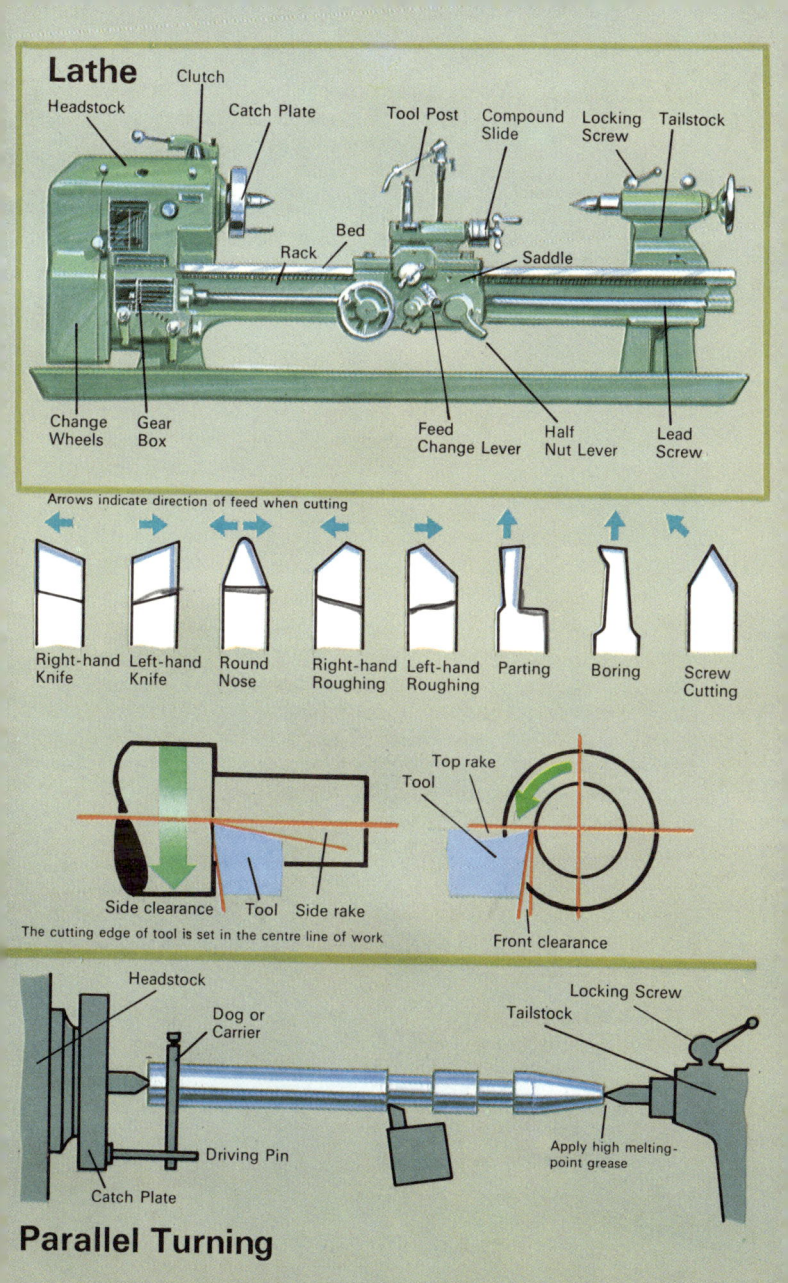

Labels: Headstock, Clutch, Catch Plate, Tool Post, Compound Slide, Locking Screw, Tailstock, Rack, Bed, Saddle, Change Wheels, Gear Box, Feed Change Lever, Half Nut Lever, Lead Screw

Arrows indicate direction of feed when cutting

- Right-hand Knife
- Left-hand Knife
- Round Nose
- Right-hand Roughing
- Left-hand Roughing
- Parting
- Boring
- Screw Cutting

Side clearance — Tool — Side rake

The cutting edge of tool is set in the centre line of work

Top rake, Tool, Front clearance

Parallel Turning

Labels: Headstock, Dog or Carrier, Locking Screw, Tailstock, Driving Pin, Catch Plate, Apply high melting-point grease

Finishing

Many metalwork jobs require some kind of surface finish to prevent tarnishing or corrosion. The kind of finish required is one of the many design considerations to be taken into account before work begins.

Work in copper, brass and gilding metal such as dishes, vases and simple jewellery need constant attention with metal polish if they are to remain bright. Colourless lacquers are available to paint or spray onto such work after it has been highly polished.

Tools of steel are often bright polished; this is achieved by drawfiling followed by emery cloth, working through the various grades from coarse to fine. Without a protective layer of oil or a lacquer coating, rust marks will appear, sooner or later.

Paints and enamels are often used to prevent metals corroding. Bridges, garden gates, washing machines and refrigerators are examples.

Taps, bathroom fittings and car bumpers are coated with non-corrosive chrome to give them a durable, good looking chromium-plated finish. In the same way dustbins and pails of steel are coated with zinc by electrolysis; this gives a dull grey galvanised finish. Tin cans, to contain foods, are made of thin sheet steel coated with a very thin layer of tin. While the tin coating remains undamaged, the steel cannot rust.

Aluminium and its alloys corrode very slowly; a special electrolytic process called *anodising* can be used to inhibit corrosion even further. Dyes can be introduced into the process which impart bright colours onto such things as kettles and saucepan lids.

Recent developments with plastics have resulted in polythene and nylon being used to coat metal objects such as vegetable racks and chain-link fencing.

Silver tarnishes and turns black if neglected, but gold, platinum and other precious metals retain their special gleam without attention.

Copper Vase – Polished, Lacquered

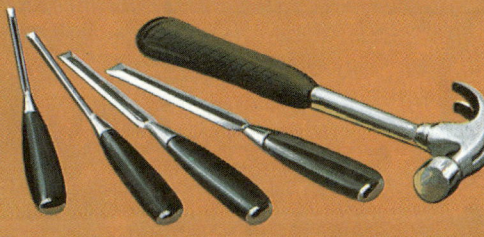

Steel Tools – Highly polished with emery

Garden Fork and Trowel – Painted

Kitchen Tap – Chrome on Brass

Dustbin – Galvanised

Saucepans – Anodised Aluminium

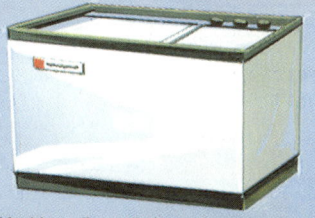

Washing Machine – Enamelled

Food Can – Tin plated

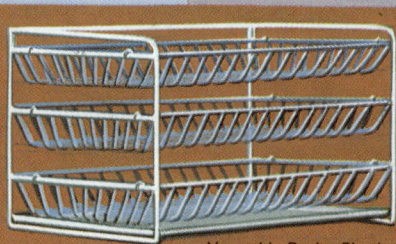

Ring – Gold

Vegetable Rack – Plastic coated

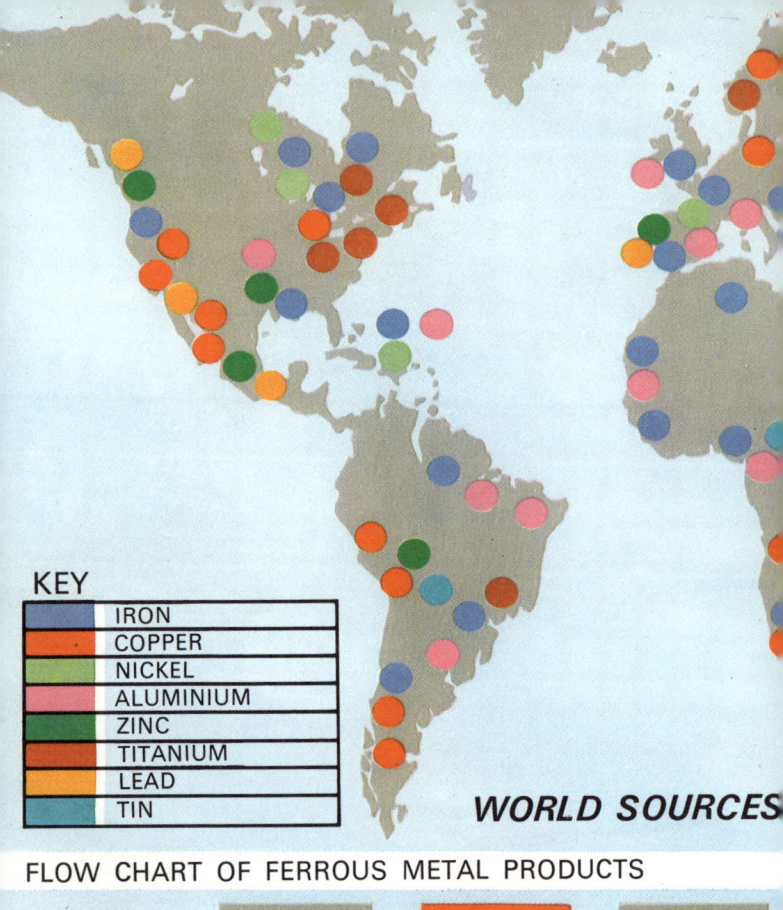

KEY

■	IRON
■	COPPER
■	NICKEL
■	ALUMINIUM
■	ZINC
■	TITANIUM
■	LEAD
■	TIN

WORLD SOURCES

FLOW CHART OF FERROUS METAL PRODUCTS

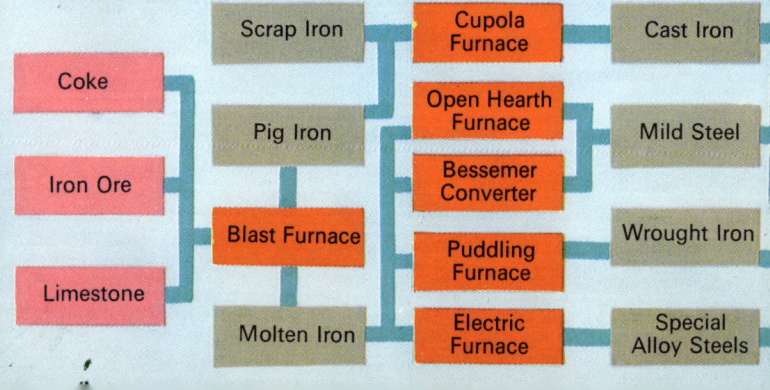

Coke	Scrap Iron	Cupola Furnace	Cast Iron
	Pig Iron	Open Hearth Furnace	Mild Steel
Iron Ore		Bessemer Converter	
	Blast Furnace	Puddling Furnace	Wrought Iron
Limestone	Molten Iron	Electric Furnace	Special Alloy Steels